Haw
BAKES

Cakes, Pies, Cookies, Biscuits and other Goodies!

with contributions from
**Mark Okumura,
Jody Domingo, Wade Tamura,
Jade Ogoshi, Kelli Kimura** *and others*

edited by **Mona Taga & Galyn Wong**

Mutual
Publishing

Library of Congress Control Number: 2012948209

ISBN-10: 1-56647-989-4
ISBN-13: 978-1-56647-989-9

All food photography © Kaz Tanabe,
    unless otherwise noted below.
From Dreamstime.com: pg. ix (upper right) ©
    Moniphoto, pg. x (upper right) © Olga Yastremska,
    pg. xi (top) © Raja Rc, pg. xiii (top) © Kabvisio,
    pg. xiii (bottom), pg. xiv (top) © Hein Schlebusch,
    pg. 3 © Enika, pg. 5 © Robert Byron, pg. 6 ©
    Rosemary Buffoni, pg. 10 © Knowlesgallery, pg.
    11 © Hdconnelly, pg. 13 © Grondin Franck Olivier,
    pg. 14 © Tim Grover, pg. 16 © Franz Schlögl, pg.
    18 © Alexander Bryljaev, pg. 19, 25 © Bert Folsom,
    pg. 24 © Homydesign, pg. 28 © Natalyw, pg. 29
    © Charles Brutlag, pg. 30 © Margo555, pg. 36
    Digitalphotonut, pg. 44 © Edith Layland, pg. 45
    © Christian Jung, pg. 47 © Nataliya Evmenenko,
    pg. 49 © Louella38, pg. 51 (both photos) © Elzbieta
    Sekowska, pg. 56 © Antpkr, pg. 57 © Viktorfischer,
    pg. 63 © Kaneos, pg. 66 © Elena Elisseeva, pg. 71
    © Julián Rovagnati, pg. 74 © Lidia Ryzhenko, pg.
    78 © John Kasawa, pg. 80 © Susan Gottberg, pg.
    81 © Olga Lyubkin, pg. 82 © Glenn Price, pg. 86 ©
    Brad Calkins, pg. 90 © Nicholas Piccillo, pg. 93 ©
    Kaycee56, pg. 95 (left) © Lcc54613, pg. 95 (right) ©
    Brad Calkins, pg. 96 © Pogonici, pg. 97 © Costasz,
    pg. 100 © Andersastphoto, pg. 104 © Justyna
    Kaminska, pg. 107 © Kontur-vid, pg. 111 © Johnny
    Lye, pg. 112 © Ari Sanjaya, pg. 116 © Marilyn
    Barbone, pg. 121 © Torsten Schon
Design by Courtney Young

Second Printing, January 2015

Mutual Publishing, LLC
1215 Center Street, Suite 210
Honolulu, Hawai'i 96816
Ph: 808-732-1709 / Fax: 808-734-4094
email: info@mutualpublishing.com
www.mutualpublishing.com

Printed in Korea

Table of Contents

Acknowledgments   vi

Introduction   viii

A Suite of Sweet Tips   xiii

SWEET STARTS

Crunchy Banana Muffins   3

Johnny Apple Scones   4

Sweet Cornmeal Muffins   5

Cinna-Yum Cinnamon Rolls   6

Cranberry Pecan Muffins   8

Forbidden Fudge Muffins   10

Some Like it HOT! Popovers   11

Simply a Biscuit   13

It's All About Sweet Sugar Biscuits   14

JUST COOKIES

Coconut Lovers Shortbread   16

Butter Shortbread Cookies   18

Mochiko Shortbread   19

Open Sesame Seed Shortbread   21

Happy Almond Cookies   22

Chocolate Chip Cookies   24

White Chocolate Chip Macadamia Nut Cookies
~ *Wade Tamura*   25

Fudge Cookies   27

Crunchy Oatmeal Cookies   28

Peanut Butter Cookies   29

Italian Tozzetti Cookies ~ *Jade Ogoshi*   30

Basler Brunsli, A Chocolate Nut Cookie   33

Chocolate Covered Sugar Cookie   34

Russian Tea Cookies   36

RAISIN' THE BAR

Fruit Squares 39
Baked Mochi with Miso 40
Easy Chi Chi Mochi 41
Wild Blondies 42
Brownie Points 44
Hot Date with Chocolate ~ *Kelli Kimura* 45
It's a Fruit Cake Bar 47
Chilly Pear Dessert 48
Pineapple Butter Sponge Bars 49
Temptin' Rugelach 50
Pumpkin Haupia Squares 52

CHARMING CUPCAKES & CAKES

Cinnamon Apple Cake 54
Easy Chocolate Coffee Mug Cake 56
Piña Colada Pound Cake 57
German Chocolate Cake 59
Pucker Up, Prune Apple Cake 60
Mango Upside Down Cake ~ *Wade Tamura* 62
Guava Marbled Cheesecake ~ *Wade Tamura* 63
Got Coffee Cake? 65
Tiramisu 66
Kalamansi Cupcake ~ *Mark Okumura* 69
Kalamansi "7 Minute" Meringue Icing 70
Peter, Peter, Pumpkin Cake 71
Red Velvet Cupcakes ~ *Mark Okumura* 72
Butter Frosting 74
Mango Cake 75
Black Forest Cake Cupcake ~ *Mark Okumura* 77
Fluffy Kirschwasser Frosting 78

PIES, TARTS & TARTLETS

Simple Pie Crust — 80
A is for Apple Pie — 81
Custard Pie — 82
Guava Frangipane Tartlets — 85
Apple Frangipane Tart — 87
Pumpkin Chiffon — 88
Haupia Chocolate Cream Pie ~ *Wade Tamura* — 90

FRESH BREAD

Jungle Monkey Bread — 93
Hot Potato Rolls — 94
Papaya Pineapple Fruit Butter — 95
Easy Beer Bread ~ *Mark Okumura* — 96
Applesauce Bread — 97
Date Nut Bread ~ *Mark Okumura* — 98
Zucchini Carrot Bread ~ *Mark Okumura* — 100

SWEET ENDINGS

Can't Let Go Cream Puffs — 103
Almond Walnut Butter Toffee — 104
Wiggle & Jiggle Coconut Gelatin — 106
Sweet Pineapple Crumble ~ *Mark Okumura* — 107
Pineapple Surprise — 109
Kula Strawberry Ice Cream ~ *Mark Okumura* — 110
Tropical Fruit Medley with Honey Yogurt Sauce — 112
Ka'a'awa Bread Pudding ~ *Jody Domingo* — 115
Vanilla Cream Sauce — 116
Hawaiian Vanilla Ice Cream ~ *Mark Okumura* — 117
Chocolate Berry Shortcake ~ *Mark Okumura* — 118
Easy Whipped Cream ~ *Mark Okumura* — 121
Fresh Berries with Vanilla Anglaise Sauce ~ *Mark Okumura* — 123
Kona Coffee Latte Gelee ~ *Mark Okumura* — 124

Glossary — 125
Recipe Index — 126
Index — 128

Acknowledgments

*M*any people contributed to this labor of love – a compilation of baked and other dessert-like delights.

Desserts, and baked ones especially, take a starring role in our "sweet" hearts. Everyone involved in making this book takes great pleasure in doing what they do best – eating them! (That's why they were chosen to be on the team.)

The assistance and TLC of our many friends to provide, evaluate, edit, or test (the best part) the recipes made this book possible as well as those who contributed to getting recipes onto the printed pages.

Special thanks to Bennett Hymer. With his encouragement and guidance, our delicious dream has become a reality. His extraordinary efforts in orchestrating the pieces of our sweet notes allowed us to compose this delightful symphony. You are an inspiration to us all.

On the design side, art director Leo Gonzalez's insights into balance colors and texture went beyond the palate, bringing out the photogenic best of scrumptious cakes, mouthwatering chocolate cookies, and all of the other goodies. Working with Kaz Tanabe, photographer extraordinaire, every dish was captured for illustration in its perfection to inspire readers to spring into action by replicating and eating these wonders.

Mutual Publishing's Courtney Young strategically understood the concept of making a cookbook entertaining, fun-filled, and colorful. She was assisted at times by over the shoulder advice from Leo Gonzalez and Jane Gillespie.

Those who shared recipes, assisted at the photo shoot, provided free advice, kibbutzed, and helped sample include:

Alfred Monico
Beverly Inoue
Charlene Kimura
Grace & Ikaika Seo
Jade Ogoshi
Jan & Robert Woodring
Jeffrey Lee
Jody & Robert Domingo
Jon & Malia Ogoshi
Justin Roberts
Kate Kincaid
Kelli Kimura

Kolohe & Bear with Lucci & Daisy
Kristy & Kari Kimura
Larry Shigaki
Laura, Steve, & Keanu Short
Leah Ramos
Linda & Carter Miller
Mark Okumura
Mia Chang
Michael Miyashiro, Rainforest
Richard Ahn
Stuart & Josie Platt
Wade Tamura

To all a heartfelt Mahalo. And let's remember the famous words of Aunty Mili:

"Eat dessert first, then the rest is all downhill."

Introduction

Sweets. You gotta love 'em. In fact, humans are hardwired to do so. And Islanders, whatever their ethnicities, are no exception. The influence of the Islands' unique ethnic and cultural blend extends to our relationship with desserts just as it does to everything else on our local-style plates. Attend an Island party and, after the soups and stews and stir-fries, there will be everything from Baked Mochi to Pineapple Surprise, Haole Brownies to Haupia Chocolate Cream Pies. Sit down and "talk story" and you'll hear about Grandma's specialties

(or Oba-chan's, Popo's or Lola's), the recipes pouring out along with the memories.

The ideas in this book came from bakers, culinary instructors, chefs and home cooks, some who prefer to remain anonymous, just as

Grandma didn't like to draw a lot of attention to herself. Grandma was best at just setting out the pie and letting you tear into it. The treats may be simple or sophisticated, easy to make or mysteriously difficult (try to master the perfect Chinese almond cookie sometime), but they are distinctly ours, influenced by the many people who have immigrated here, as well as the abundance of fruits and nuts that populate the Islands.

It begins, of course, with sugar — not just a commercial crop that became the Islands' No. 1 industry for a period, but a staple that was already here, lovingly transported in the canoes of the first settlers from the South Pacific.

Though Hawaiians had no metals with which to make conventional pots, pans or stoves, they had kō, sugar, which they used both as food and as a windbreak to protect their fields and mark their boundaries. And although they did not refine sugar in the modern sense, they did cut the stalks, mash and grind them with stones and squeeze out the sweet juice by hand.

They would use this ingredient in making such dishes as the ancestor of today's popular, cornstarch-based haupia pudding. Their recipe was simple: fresh coconut cream, sugar cane juice and grated arrowroot, bound up in leaves and steamed in an imu, or earth oven. They also made a taro-based steamed coconut pudding called kulolo, which is still a great labor of love because grating taro is hard work!

People of all ages gnawed on stalks of cane as they ambled from here to there, just as many of today's adults recall doing in plantation times, before folks could afford store-bought candy bars.

In the 1800s, explorers, missionaries, merchants and other adventurers brought with them both the technique for processing sugar and a world of ingredients with which to combine it.

Until the post-WWII years, sweets as we know them today were most often enjoyed only in the most privileged homes. Sugar, flour, butter, eggs, chocolate, spices and such were too expensive for working-class families.

Still, the melting pot was already beginning its work. The cooks who served in rich kitchens learned to prepare and savor everything from penuche to pecan pie, even if they had grown up in households that knew nothing of these Western-style delights. Naturally, a hunger for Western-style goods soon developed. Ask any plantation-era elder and they will speak with longing of the special occasions when their parents would splurge on a can of sweetened, condensed milk and they'd spread it on bread. The rarity of these things seems to have made them all the sweeter. But it was not only the privileged Westerners who packed their confectionary "receipts" with them when they came here. Other cultures did, too.

Chinese brought "mui" (seed), a sprawling family of sweet and salty preserved fruits, doled out at tiny neighborhood stores from glass confectioners' jars. We called all of them "crack seed," although somewhat confusing to newcomers, mui may or may not contain seeds and the seeds may or may not be cracked. Today, store-bought or homemade soft, sweet, seedless fruit mui — prune or apricot, for example — are often used in place of candied fruits to make tender cakes or bar cookies. The "li hing" spice mixture that flavors many types of mui is blended into recipes that might once have been flavored with cinnamon or other spices.

Japanese and Okinawans brought "mochi," a family of puffy and delicate steamed confections, based on mochiko, or rice flour. At first, mochi makers kept to their accustomed ways, preparing small cakes of rice flour, water, sugar and flavorings, perhaps softly tinted with colored foodstuffs and stuffed with mashed, sweetened beans.

But those traditional confections soon met up with ingredients not routinely used in Japan at that time. One result: butter mochi, a sort of rice flour fudge prized by all Islanders.

Portuguese, many of whom became dairymen and most of whom kept a chicken or two as soon as they could afford it, brought a love of anything based on butter and eggs, particular pao doce (sweet bread), malasadas (holeless doughnuts), puddings and custards.

Did the rather thin and savory Japanese egg-based custard called chawan mushi somehow cross the path of the richer milk custard made by Portuguese hands, and then land in a plateful of Western-style pastry to become one of Hawaii's all-time favorite desserts, custard pie?

Filipinos, too, brought their sweets — biko, bibingka and others, based on glutinous rice, sweet potato, tapioca and other starches, cooked with coconut milk and sugar and other flavorings. Coming from an already blended culture, Filipinos also extended our menu of flour-based breads, cakes and rolls.

In many ways, you can see all these dishes on a continuum that begins with haupia and kulolo and travels right through mochi cakes and butter mochi, biko and bibingka to muffins, shortbread, scones, cookies and other Western-style baked goods.

And you gotta love 'em.

A Suite of Sweet Tips

* Arm yourself with GOOD TOOLS: high-quality bake ware, cooking thermometers (instant-read and candy), Silpat sheets, kitchen parchment, accurate measuring tools including a kitchen scale, Micro-plane graters, sharp knives.

* Always PREHEAT THE OVEN as a first step.

* READ THE RECIPE CAREFULLY; line up all ingredients, measured and ready to use.

* "GREASE" baking tools with baking sprays; or use the softened butter clinging to the wrapper.

* "CREAM" in baking means to beat briskly in a circular motion until the fat "mounts" the sugar and becomes lighter-colored, with more volume.

* To "FOLD" is not to "stir." Gently spoon light mixture onto heavier batter; use a rubber spatula in a side-to-side circular motion, lifting the heavier mixture up and over the lighter mixture.

* OVER MIXING is the enemy of tender baked goods, particularly muffins, biscuits, pastries and mixtures leavened with egg and/ or egg white. With muffins, for example, a few swift turns and you're done.

* The other enemy: WARMTH. Keep pastry shortening solid and chilled, refrigerate beaters and bowl before whipping cream, don't work mixture so long that fats begin to melt.

* To CHECK FOR DONENESS: Insert a toothpick, skewer or knife in center; it should emerge clean (a few moist crumbs are okay). Internal temperature of baked goods, measured on an instant-read thermometer, should be: cheesecakes and custards, 150-160 degrees; crusty breads, 210 degrees; sweet breads, 195 degrees; cakes and quick breads, 190-195; brownies or other moist baked goods, 170 degrees.

* Wherever possible, use FRESH rather than canned fruit. If fruit needs to be soft and liquid, cook it briefly in sugared water or agave syrup.

* CRAISINS are sweetened, dried cranberries; useful to have around and available in large bags in box stores.

* Throughout, "VANILLA" means pure vanilla extract (not imitation) and "SUGAR" means white, granulated sugar.

sweetstarts

Eating breakfast daily — even if you prefer to get going
first and eat mid-morning — is an earmark of a healthful
diet. But the morning meal needn't be a penitential bowl of
"weeds and straw" every day. Breakfast breads generally
take just a short amount of time to make. Quick breads such
as muffins can be prepared in advance, refrigerated and
nibbled as you drive to work. Many quick breads also freeze
well and can be doled out as you need them. Yeast breads
can be set to rise in the refrigerator at night, then baked in
the morning to be slathered with butter.
Start with these sweet treats.

Crunchy Banana Muffins

Hawaiians knew bananas as a starch — more a potato than a fruit, to be steamed and eaten with meat and fish. After Western contact, more than 150 varieties made their way here. For this muffin with its crunchy nut topping, use conventional "Chiquita" or try sweet-tart apple bananas (they're smaller, so increase number to two bananas).

For the muffins:
¾ cup butter (1½ sticks), room temperature
1½ cups brown sugar
2 eggs
1½ ripe bananas, slightly mashed
1 teaspoon baking soda
1 teaspoon baking powder
2 cups all-purpose flour
1 teaspoon vanilla

For the topping:
½ cup brown sugar
1 teaspoon cinnamon
½ cup walnuts, chopped

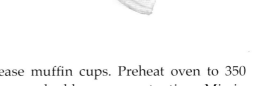

Make the muffin batter: Grease muffin cups. Preheat oven to 350 degrees. Cream butter and sugar and add eggs, one at a time. Mix in remaining ingredients.

Make the topping: Mix together sugar, cinnamon and chopped walnuts.

Assemble: Scoop batter into greased muffin cups, placing topping on top of batter before baking at 350 degrees for 30 minutes.

Variation: *Replace walnuts with macadamias.*

Johnny Apple Scones

Low-calorie, high-fiber apples, with their antioxidant powers, make all the Top 20 lists of nutritional "super fruits." For cooking, such as this apple version of a traditional strawberry shortcake, choose firm varieties with sugar and acid well-balanced, such as Fuji.

For the filling:
   1 apple, peeled, cored, diced
   1 tablespoon sugar
   ¼ teaspoon cinnamon

For the scones:
   2 cups all-purpose flour
   1 tablespoon baking powder
   1 teaspoon cinnamon
   ¼ cup sugar
   ¼ cup unsalted butter (½ stick), chilled and cubed
   ¾ cup heavy cream (more, as needed)

Make filling: Toss diced apple with sugar and cinnamon; place in microwave-safe bowl; heat 1 minute, then allow to cool. Set aside.

Make the dough: In the bowl of a food processor fitted with a metal blade, combine flour, baking powder, cinnamon and sugar; pulse to mix. Add chilled butter and pulse on and off until dough becomes crumbly. While processor is running, drizzle in heavy cream. Process just until dough forms a ball; do not over mix.

Remove dough from food processor. Pinch off golf ball-sized pieces of dough, pull edges to form a disc; fill with about 1 tablespoon apple filling. Wrap edges around apple filling, placing seam-side-down on cookie sheet.

Bake at 425 degrees for 12-15 minutes until golden brown. Remove from baking pan onto a wire rack and cool.

Variations: *Use pears, bananas, strawberries or blueberries (fresh or frozen, defrosted).*

Sweet Cornmeal Muffins

YIELD: 16 PIECES

Islanders love sweet cornbread, a style that would never fly in the South. Nevertheless, it makes an easy-to-pack breakfast and goes well with chili and stews, too. For more flavor and fiber, use a less processed, medium-grind cornmeal, such as that available from Bob's Red Mill.

1 cup sugar
½ cup butter, slightly softened
2 eggs
½ teaspoon baking powder
2 cups Bisquick
1 cup milk
2 tablespoons yellow cornmeal

With an electric mixer or by hand, cream together sugar and butter. Beat in eggs one at a time, then alternate dry and wet ingredients. Stir in cornmeal. Pour into greased muffin cups.

Bake at 350 degrees for 25-30 minutes.

Variation: *Use a 9 by 9-inch pan instead of muffin cups, increasing baking time to 35-40 minutes.*

Cinna-Yum
Cinnamon Rolls

*Everybody loves those commercial Cinna-you-know-whats, but with a little
flour magic, you can make your own. The secret is a combination of low-
gluten cake flour (or use Southern-style biscuit flour) and high-gluten bread
flour, both available in grocery stores. All-purpose is acceptable
but the rolls won't be as light.*

For the dough:
1½ teaspoons dry yeast
1 cup milk
1 cup cake flour
3 cups bread flour
1 teaspoon salt
¼ cup sugar
2 eggs
⅓ cup melted butter
1 teaspoon vanilla
½ cup (1 stick) softened butter

For the filling:
1 egg, beaten
1 cup sugar
2 tablespoons cinnamon
2 cups raisins, golden or dark

For the glaze:
½ cup sugar (fine baking sugar, if you've got it)
2 tablespoons hot water (possibly more)

Make the dough: Heat ¼ cup of the milk to lukewarm. Sprinkle yeast over milk, stir to dissolve and allow to proof (2-3 minutes). Combine remaining dry ingredients, add liquid ingredients and yeast mixture. Knead dough for 10 minutes. Roll dough out on floured surface, spread softened butter over half of the dough. Fold unbuttered side over the buttered surface. Turn dough one quarter-turn and roll out again. Fold dough in thirds (similar to folding a letter). Place dough in bowl, cover with plastic wrap and refrigerate for several hours.

Make the filling and reserve: Combine egg, sugar, cinnamon. Keep raisins in reserve.

Make the glaze and reserve: Whisk together sugar and hot water until sugar dissolves.

Remove chilled dough and roll out, fold in thirds, give quarter-turn and roll into an 18 by 18-inch square. Brush beaten egg over dough. Sprinkle sugar/cinnamon mixture over egg. Top with raisins.

Roll dough to form a log, then cut in 9 equal slices.

Place rolls in 9 by 13-inch baking pan lined with parchment paper. Try to leave space between rolls, they will expand. Place in warm area, allow to rise and double in size (approximately 1 hour).

Bake at 325 degrees for 25 minutes until lightly brown.

Variations: *In place of plain raisins, combine raisins, nuts, Craisins (sugared, dried cranberries) or other dehydrated fruit, chopped.*

Cranberry Pecan Muffins

YIELD: 30 MUFFINS

When fresh cranberries are available around Christmas, throw a few bags in the freezer so you can make these sweet-tart-nutty muffins year-round. Cranberries are naturally low in fat and high in fiber. If you like, cut the sugar load with a substitute such as Splenda, which can be substituted 1-for-1 for the sugar in this recipe.

1½ cups whole cranberries, fresh or frozen, coarsely chopped
¼ cup sugar
3 cups sifted all-purpose flour
4½ teaspoons baking powder
½ teaspoon salt
1 cup sugar
½ cup vegetable shortening
1 cup pecans, chopped
2 teaspoons lemon zest
2 eggs
1 cup milk

Combine cranberries and ¼ cup sugar in a small bowl. Set aside.

Sift flour, baking powder, salt and sugar into a large bowl. Cut shortening into flour mixture until crumbly. Stir in pecans and lemon zest. Beat eggs in a small bowl and stir in milk. Add liquid to flour mixture, stirring until moist. Fold in cranberry mixture. Spoon into greased muffin cups, about two-thirds full. Bake at 400 degrees for 20 minutes until golden brown. Remove from muffin pans and cool on wire rack. Serve warm.

Variation: *Try walnuts or macadamia nuts.*

Forbidden Fudge Muffins

YIELD: 36 MUFFINS

The Italians would say these muffins "put a base on your stomach"; they're dense and moist with no leavening to lighten them. Break the chocolate into uniform pieces for even melting; substitute dark, high cacao-fat semi-sweet chocolate, if you like.

2 cups unsalted butter
8 ounces sweet baking chocolate
3½ cups sugar
2 cups sifted unbleached all-purpose flour
Pinch salt
8 eggs
2 teaspoons vanilla
4 cups chopped nuts
36 nut halves (pecans or walnuts)

Melt butter with chocolate in a double boiler set over simmering water or in the microwave. Sift flour, then measure the 2 cups from the sifted flour. Combine sugar, flour and salt in large bowl. Stir in chocolate mixture. Add eggs and vanilla; whisk until ingredients are evenly moistened, but do not over-mix. Fold in nuts. Spoon batter in lined muffin cups, fill two-thirds full. Top each with one whole nut. Bake muffins at 300 degrees for 40 minutes, until tester inserted in center comes out clean. Cool on wire rack.

Variation: *Try macadamia nuts.*

Some Like it HOT!
Popovers

Airy popovers rely on steam trapped in the thin, egg-rich batter and should always be served hot. Use custard cups rather than muffin tins; they're deeper and hold more batter for a higher rise.

2 eggs, room temperature
1 cup whole milk
1 tablespoon melted butter
1 cup sifted all-purpose flour
½ teaspoon salt

Preheat oven to 425 degrees. Beat eggs until frothy with electric mixer or hand beater. Stir in milk and melted butter; beat until blended. Beat in flour and salt until batter is smooth. Grease each custard cup with salad oil. Place on a baking sheet in preheated oven. When the oil in the custard cups start smoking, remove from the oven. Then pour in the batter, filling each about half full as quickly as possible to prevent the loss of heat from the custard cups. Place back in the oven and bake. Bake at 425 degrees for 25-35 minutes. Remove from oven, cut slit in each popover to allow steam to escape, return to oven and bake 5 minutes longer, or until popover is deep brown and very crisp.

Simply a Biscuit

Biscuits have a reputation for being tricky. Words to live by: Soft, low-gluten flour (buy White Lily online or use part cake flour); hard, cold shortening (butter, vegetable shortening, and margarine) and keep your need-to-knead hands off!

1¾ cups cake flour
3 teaspoons baking powder
½ teaspoon salt
2 tablespoons sugar
1 egg, beaten
½ cup shortening
¼ cup milk
1 tablespoon butter,
   melted

Preheat oven to 350 degrees. Sift together flour, baking powder, salt and sugar, set aside. Cream shortening and egg in mixing bowl. Add dry ingredients and mix until crumbly. Stir in milk until just combined. Be careful not to overwork the dough. Pour batter on floured table and roll out with a rolling pin to approximately ½-inch thick. Cut into desired size and brush tops with melted butter. Allow to rise, approximately 15-30 minutes. Bake until golden brown. Bake at 350 degrees for 15-20 minutes.

Variations:

❉ *Add ½ cup shredded cheddar.*

❉ *Add ½ cup shredded cheddar with jalapeño. Use canned or jarred as they are partially cooked and ready to use.*

It's All About
Sweet Sugar Biscuits

If you think savory when you think biscuits, think again. This light-textured version balances a bit of sweetness (sugar on top) with the bite of fresh-ground nutmeg — a perfect pairing with egg dishes.

2½ cups all-purpose flour
1 teaspoon baking powder
¼ teaspoon salt
Pinch nutmeg, freshly grated
½ cup unsalted butter (1 stick)
¾ cup sugar
2 tablespoons milk
1 egg
1 teaspoon vanilla
2 tablespoons sugar for sprinkling

Sift together flour, baking powder, salt and nutmeg. Cream butter and sugar. Stir in milk, egg and vanilla. Blend in dry ingredients. Roll dough into a 1½-2-inch log. Wrap with plastic wrap. Chill until very firm. Remove plastic wrap; cut log into ⅛-inch slices. Transfer to ungreased baking sheets spacing about 2 inches apart. Press fork tines into edges of slices to decorate, dipping fork in cold water if necessary to prevent sticking. Sprinkle centers of slices with 2 tablespoons sugar. Bake at 375 degrees 8-10 minutes, until edges begin to color. Cool on wire racks.

justcookies

"If you give a mouse a cookie," as the children's story delightfully tell us … he'll just want another, as we all do. Whether you call it a biscuit or, belovedly, "bikkie," as they do in Great Britain, or a cookie, as we do in the U.S., it's small, it's portable, it's at least somewhat sweet, it's made with some kind of flour and it's a treat nearly impossible to refuse. Baking cookies together is a particularly enjoyable way to introduce children to the kitchen. And you end with two sorts of sweetness: togetherness and warm cookies!

Coconut Lovers Shortbread

YIELD: 5-6 DOZEN

This recipe may or may not have been invented in the Islands, but it made its appearance in many community cookbooks in the mid-20th century, when flaked, sweetened coconut became widely available, and hasn't stopped pleasing us since. An added bonus: Coconut's fats are the "good" kind and coconut contains healthful fiber.

2 cups (4 sticks) butter
1 cup sugar
4 cups all-purpose flour
3½ ounces sweetened shredded coconut

Cream butter and sugar, then add flour. Stir in coconut. Form in 2-inch diameter logs, cover with plastic wrap and chill in refrigerator. Slice ¼-inch thick and place on baking sheet. Bake at 325 degrees for 25-30 minutes. Cool on rack. Roll in powdered sugar if desired.

Butter Shortbread Cookies

YIELD: 24

Shortbread is one of those classic recipes that separate the good cooks from the also-rans: with a little butter, sugar, flour and flavoring, there are no frills to hide behind. It's a simple cookie with very few ingredients, so it's how you measure, mix and handle the dough that compares a good cookie to an excellent cookie. Your proportions must be right, and your handling deft and swift.

2 cups all-purpose flour
1 cup butter (2 sticks)
1 cup sugar
1 egg, separated
½ cup macadamia nuts, chopped

Cream butter and sugar, beat in egg yolk, and add flour. Divide dough in half; place pieces on two rimmed cookie sheets and press with fingers and rolling pin to cover ¼-inch thick. Beat egg whites until foamy and brush dough with beaten egg white. Sprinkle nuts on top. Bake at 375 degrees for 20-25 minutes. Cut immediately into squares and remove from pan.

Mochiko Shortbread

*Who first had the idea of using mochiko — sweet or glutinous rice flour —
instead of wheat flour in Western-style goods? We cannot know but "butter
mochi" recipes have proliferated in the last quarter-century.
Here, mochiko offers snappy crispness but all-purpose flour
is needed for a tender crumb.*

2 cups (4 sticks) butter, softened
1½ cups sugar
2 teaspoons pure vanilla extract
2 teaspoons baking soda
3 cups all-purpose flour
1 cup mochiko
1 cup macadamia nuts, chopped (optional)

Preheat oven to 350 degrees. Cream butter and sugar until light and
fluffy. Add vanilla. Mix well. Add baking soda, flour, mochiko and
chopped nuts, if using; blend well. Drop by rounded teaspoonfuls
onto cookie sheet and bake at 350 degrees for 15-20 minutes or until
slightly golden.

Open Sesame Seed Shortbread

YIELD: 18 COOKIES

Yet another shortbread, but this time the recipes showcases one of the longest known edible condiments, the sesame seed, which originated in India. Toast the seeds before you use them: 10 minutes in a 325-degree oven, shaken frequently.

½ cup butter (1 stick)
½ cup sugar
1 egg
2 cups all-purpose flour
½ teaspoon baking powder
3 tablespoons toasted sesame seeds
1 egg, separated

Preheat oven to 350 degrees.

Cream butter and sugar until light and fluffy. Add egg and mix well. Sift flour and baking powder; add to creamed mixture.

Form dough into walnut-size balls and place on ungreased cookie sheet. Flatten to ¼-inch thickness. Beat egg yolk and brush over cookies. Sprinkle with sesame seeds and press firmly, then brush with egg whites. Bake at 350 degrees for 12-15 minutes.

Happy Almond Cookies

YIELD: 30-36 COOKIES

The perfect almond cookie shatters when you bite into it, melts to nothing as soon as it touches your tongue and leaves just a trace of sweet almond flavor. The secret is cold, hard shortening; try frozen Crisco. Add a red dot with the end of a chopstick for good fortune.

1½ cups shortening
1¼ cups sugar
1 egg
3 cups all-purpose flour
1 teaspoon salt
1 teaspoon baking soda
2 teaspoons pure almond extract
Red food coloring

Preheat oven to 325 degrees. Cream shortening and sugar, then add egg and almond extract. Blend dry ingredients and mix into shortening mixtures. Shape dough into rough, 1-inch-diameter balls; flatten into discs. Dust your thumb with flour and make an impression in the center of each cookie. Dot each center with red food coloring. Bake at 325 degrees for 12 minutes.

Chocolate Chip Cookies

YIELD: 24 (4-INCH) COOKIES

Forget apple pie. Chocolate chip cookies — as invented at the original Toll House Inn in Whitman, Mass. by Ruth Graves Wakefield — are the quintessential American sweet. Making chocolate cookies, Wakefield ran out of baking chocolate and used chopped-up semi-sweet instead, learning accidentally that the chips wouldn't melt.

2 cups all-purpose flour
1 teaspoon baking soda
1 teaspoon salt
1 cup butter (2 sticks)
1½ cups sugar
1 egg
1 teaspoon vanilla
1 package semi-sweet chocolate chips (12 ounces)
1 cup macadamia nuts

Preheat oven to 350 degrees. Combine flour, baking soda and salt; set aside. In large mixing bowl, cream butter and gradually beat in sugar until light. Beat in egg and vanilla. Stir in flour mixture, chocolate and nuts. Shape into 2-inch balls, and place 3 inches apart on ungreased baking sheets (six on each sheet). Bake at 350 degrees for 20-25 minutes.

Variations: *Try pecans or walnuts.*

White Chocolate Macadamia Nut Cookies

You know the drill: White chococolate isn't chocolate; it's cocoa butter or "white confectionary". Whatever you call it, it's got a dreamy, creamy texture as exemplified in these cookies.

2¼ cups all-purpose flour
1 teaspoon baking soda
½ teaspoon salt
1 cup butter (2 sticks)
1 cup light brown sugar
½ cup sugar
2 eggs, room-temperature
1 teaspoon vanilla
3½ cups macadamia nuts, chopped
2½ cups white chocolate chips

Preheat oven to 350 degrees. In a medium bowl, whisk together flour, baking soda and salt; set aside. In a stand mixer fitted with a paddle attachment, cream together butter, brown sugar and sugar. Add eggs one at a time, followed by vanilla extract. Stir in flour and mix until almost all incorporated, then mix in nuts and chocolate. Scoop dough into 1-inch balls and place 2 inches apart onto a baking sheet. Bake at 350 degrees for 12-15 minutes.

Fudge Cookies

YIELD: 30-36 COOKIES

Love brownies but don't want to mess with a baking pan and cutting perfect squares? Earn brownie points with this soft chocolate icebox cookie. Icebox cookies are so-called because you chill the dough so that it firms up and holds its shape when you slice it. Make round logs or, if you like, pat and shape the dough into rectangles for square cookies.

2½ cups semi-sweet chocolate chips
14 ounces sweetened condensed milk
3 tablespoons unsalted butter
2 cups all-purpose flour
½ teaspoon baking soda
1 teaspoon vanilla extract
½ cup chopped nuts

In medium saucepan, combine chocolate chips, sweetened condensed milk and butter. Cook over low heat, stirring, until chocolate is melted. Remove from heat. Add remaining ingredients. Mix well. Divide dough into thirds. Shape each into an 8-inch log. Wrap in plastic wraps and chill until firm, 2-hour minimum. Preheat oven to 350 degrees. Cut chilled logs into ¼-inch slices and place on ungreased baking sheets. Bake at 350 degrees for 7-9 minutes until tops are slightly crusted. Cool 2-3 minutes before removing from baking sheets. Pack in tightly covered containers.

Variations: *Use all or mixed — walnuts, pecans, almonds, macadamia nuts, white chocolate chips.*

Crunchy Oatmeal Cookies

YIELD: 36-40 COOKIES

Old-fashioned is as old-fashioned tastes in these cookies made with rolled oats (whole oats steamed and flattened into flakes to cook more quickly). Cholesterol-fighting oats are the heart of this crunchy cookie; adding other ingredients, such as fruits and nuts, makes a more chewy type.

1 cup butter
1 cup sugar
1 egg
2½ cups all-purpose flour
1 teaspoon baking soda
½ teaspoon salt
2 cups old-fashioned rolled oats or quick oats
Powdered sugar (for rolling, optional)

Preheat oven to 350 degrees. Cream butter and sugar then add egg. Combine flour, baking soda and salt. Stir into butter mixture mix until combined. Stir in oats. Roll dough into balls and flatten. Bake at 350 degrees for 20 minutes. If desired, roll in powdered sugar while warm.

Variations: *Add raisins, shredded coconut, Craisins, dried cranberries, chopped dates, chocolate chips.*

Peanut Butter Cookies

YIELD: 36 COOKIES

The introduction of commercial peanut butter led to this beautifully homogenized cookie (previous peanut cookies were butter cookies with crushed or chopped nuts mixed in). Use chunky or creamy, natural or hydrogenated. Don't forget the criss-cross on top!

½ cup butter (1 stick)
½ cup peanut butter
½ cup sugar
½ cup brown sugar
1 egg
1½ cups all-purpose flour
1 teaspoon baking soda
¼ teaspoon salt

Preheat oven to 325 degrees. Cream butter and peanut butter until well blended. Add sugars; blend. Add egg. Mix in dry ingredients. Shape into balls, flatten and make crisscross pattern with a fork.

Bake at 325 degrees for 12 minutes.

Italian Tozzetti Cookies

YIELD: 120 PIECES

Tozzetti are a Roman-style hazelnut-almond biscotti; toast that has gone uptown. These are easy because, unlike conventional biscotti, you bake them only once and you needn't chop the nuts.

Jade Ogoshi savored this rustic cookie while in Vetralla, central Italy, from her home-stay family; Aldo, Mamma Rita and Aurora.

6⅛ cups flour
½ teaspoon baking powder
1 tablespoon cinnamon
1⅓ sticks butter
Scant 2⅛ cups sugar
3 eggs
1.4 ounces Disaronno Amaretto Liqueur
1 egg lightly beaten for glazing
4½ cups hazelnuts

Preheat oven to 350 degrees. Sift flour, baking powder, and cinnamon together. Melt butter, add sugar, eggs, and amaretto liqueur. Mix butter mixture and hazelnuts. Work flour mixture in to make pliable dough. Roll out into finger-width logs on floured surface. Cut into 3-inch lengths. Pinch dough around hazelnuts, using left and right hands. Beat additional egg. Brush egg on each tozzetti to glaze. Bake at 350 degrees on ungreased pans for 50 minutes.

Basler Brunsli,
A Chocolate Nut Cookie

YIELD: 32 COOKIES

This traditional Swiss Christmas cookie needn't wait for December. Use your choice of ground almonds, hazelnuts, pecans, walnuts or a combination. (Buy nuts as fresh as you can; store in the freezer in an airtight container; use within two months.)

1½ cups almonds, ground very fine
1½ cups sugar
3 tablespoons cocoa powder (¾ oz)
3 egg whites, slightly beaten
2 tablespoons corn syrup
Pinch cinnamon
¼ teaspoon lemon zest

Combine almonds and sugar in the food processor, pulsing till mixture is finely ground. In a mixing bowl, combine cocoa powder and ground almond mixture; add the egg whites and corn syrup, pinch of cinnamon and lemon zest. Combine all ingredients well to incorporate. Refrigerate for an hour or overnight.

Preheat oven to 350 degrees. Drop dough by spoonful on a baking sheet lined with parchment paper. Give cookies room as they will spread. Bake at 350 degrees until set but not hard; about 8 minutes. Cookies should be crisp on the outside and chewy on the inside.

Chocolate Covered Sugar Cookies

Here, sugar cookies put on a "tuxedo" of chocolate with chopped apricot embellishments, a traditional combination in Eastern Europe.

1 cup unsalted butter
1 cup sugar
1 egg
¼ teaspoon salt
2 teaspoons pure vanilla extract
2⅔ cups all-purpose flour
8 ounces semi-sweet or dark chocolate
½ cup chopped apricots

Cream butter, sugar, egg, salt and vanilla. Beat well. Add flour to combine. Chill dough. Roll out and cut into desired shape. Bake at 375 degrees for 15-20 minutes and cool cookies.

Melt chocolate and coat cooled cookie, using a small frosting palette or butter knife; sprinkle with chopped apricots while chocolate is still warm, pressing slightly into chocolate and allowing chocolate to set. Alternately, you may stir apricots into the melted chocolate and spread over cooled cookie. Allow chocolate to set completely before storing.

Russian Tea Cookies

YIELD: 72 COOKIES

Known variously as Russian Tea Cookies, Nut Butter Balls, Mexican Wedding Cakes, Melting Moments, Danish Almond Cookies and Snowballs, these sugar-dusted cookies date back hundreds of years. The better quality the walnuts, the better the cookie.

2 cups butter (4 sticks)
1 cup powdered sugar or confectioner's sugar
½ teaspoon vanilla extract
¼ teaspoon salt
4 cups all-purpose flour
½ cup walnuts, chopped
Powdered sugar for dusting

Preheat oven to 300 degrees. Cream butter and powdered sugar, then add vanilla extract and salt. Slowly add flour and nuts. Mix until just combined. Scoop into balls on a cookie sheet. Bake at 300 degrees for 12-15 minutes until edges brown. Immediately toss in powdered sugar and cool on wire rack.

Variations: *Use almonds or pecans.*

raisin'the bar

This chapter is a happy marriage.

First, all the recipes use fresh or dried fruit or nuts for sweetness and flavor. We've all heard it: Eat fruit and nuts for sugars that are more slowly released, fats that aren't bad for you, and for fiber. Here are some pleasant ways to follow that advice.

Plus, most of these recipes are bar- or brownie-type cookies that don't take a lot of portioning, cutting or shaping. The exception is the rugelach beloved of all fans of Jewish baked goods; these take a little work but, trust us, they're worth it!

Fruit Squares

This quick-together bar cookie makes use of canned fruit pie filling, always available in the supermarket. The versatile crust can be used for other bar cookies such as the classic lemon bar. Or, in place of the pie filling, use a good quality, whole-fruit jam or, at Christmas time, use a jar of mincemeat.

For the filling:
1 (20-ounce) can fruit filling (cherry, blueberry)
1 cup sugar

For the crust:
1¾ cups sugar
5 cups all-purpose flour
2½ cups butter (5 sticks)
5 egg yolks

Preheat oven to 375 degrees. Mix flour and sugar. Cut in butter, then mix in egg yolks. Crust will be crumbly. Press half of the crust in bottom of baking pan. Spread fruit filling over bottom crust. Crumble remaining crust on top of fruit filling. Bake at 375 degrees for 30 minutes or until top crust is golden brown.

Tip: Ready-to-use apple fruit filling may need a bit more sugar and a touch of cinnamon for a successful bar. If using apple fruit filling, drain liquid, heat in a small saucepan with 1 tablespoon sugar and ½ teaspoon cinnamon, stirring for 3 minutes. Cool before mixing in the 1 cup of sugar in the recipe.

Baked Mochi with Miso

Miso adds a salty tang to these cakes served during Japanese festivals and on special occasions. A dusting of kinako (soy bean flour) or katakuriko (potato starch) keeps the sticky delights separated and easy to handle.

1 box mochi flour (1 pound)
2¼ cups sugar
1 can coconut milk (12 ounces), thawed if frozen
2 cups water
1 tablespoon white miso
20-25 drops red food coloring, if desired
Kinako (soybean flour) or katakuriko (potato starch)

Preheat oven to 350 degrees. Combine mochi flour and sugar in a large bowl. Make a well in the center. Combine milk, water and miso. Add to dry ingredients, mix well using a wire whisk. Add food coloring (if desired). Pour mixture into a well-greased baking pan. Cover completely with foil. Bake at 350 degrees for 1 hour, 15 minutes.

Important: Cool mochi for at least 10-12 hours. Cut mochi into strips with a plastic knife and gently pull out of pan. Slice and roll mochi in kinako or katakuriko.

Variation: *For tri-color mochi, divide filling into thirds (approximately 2½ cups each) in separate bowls. To the first bowl, add 5-6 drops of red food coloring. To the second bowl, add 5-6 drops green food coloring. Then the last bowl 8 drops of yellow food coloring.*

Bake first layer 20 minutes, then pour the second layer over the first layer in the pan. Return to oven and continue baking second layer for 20 minutes, then pour the last layer over the top and return to oven. Continue baking last layer 30 minutes.

Easy Chi Chi Mochi

YIELD: 20 PIECES

The texture of mochi cakes is likened to the softness of a woman's breast in the term "chichidango." This version takes the guesswork out by use of a mochi mold (try Don Quijote, Marukai or any Japanese grocer or household store), a plastic pan with a hole in the center, rather like a tube cake pan, to allow the mochi to cook right through to the center.

1 cup mochiko flour
¾ cup sugar
3 tablespoons coconut milk, canned or frozen
1 cup hot water
1 drop food coloring
Katakuriko (potato starch)

Whisk together mochiko flour and sugar. Mix in the coconut milk and the hot water. Spray or grease your mochi mold. Pour mixture into the mold. Microwave on high for 5 minutes. Cool and cut with a plastic knife into ½-inch pieces. Dust with potato starch to prevent sticking.

Wild Blondies

YIELD: 8 BY 8-INCH PAN

Blondies — known in Hawai'i as Haole Brownies — are chocolate-less, butterscotch-flavored brownies. Nuts and light brown sugar lend these an earthy, molasses flavor. Dried wild blueberries and Craisins (sugared, dried cranberries) balance the sweetness and add a touch of fiber, too.

1¼ cups all-purpose flour
1½ cups light brown sugar (lightly packed)
1½ teaspoons baking powder
⅛ teaspoon salt
2 eggs, room temperature
10 tablespoons melted unsalted butter, cooled
2 teaspoons vanilla extract
½ cups chopped walnuts
¼ cup dried wild blueberries
¼ cup Craisins

Preheat oven to 350 degrees. Mix flour, brown sugar, baking powder and salt in medium size bowl; set aside. Beat eggs with a whisk and blend in melted butter and vanilla. Make a well in dry ingredients and pour in the egg mixture. Using a spoon, stir until mixture is blended. Add walnuts, wild blueberries, Craisins and spread evenly into greased pan. Bake at 350 degrees for 35-40 minutes until golden and feels firm to touch. Place pan on wire rack for an hour to cool before cutting.

Variation: *Use pecans or macadamia nuts.*

Brownie Points

*Build a better brownie by using the best chocolate you can afford. Preceed
your baking experience with a side by side tasting of the many high cacao-fat
unsweetened chocolates now sold in supermarkets and specialty stores, to
find the flavor your crave. Dark chocolate has delightful health side effects,
including helping to lower cholesterol, and smoothing
out the metabolism of sugars.*

1½ cups all-purpose flour
½ teaspoon baking powder
½ teaspoon salt
6 ounces unsweetened chocolate (6 squares)
1 cup unsalted butter, 2 sticks
2 cups sugar
4 eggs
1 teaspoon vanilla extract
1½ cups walnuts, chopped

Preheat oven to 350 degrees. Grease or oil-spray
a 9 by 13-inch pan. Mix flour, baking powder
and salt in a bowl. Set aside. Melt chocolate
and butter in a large saucepan over low
heat. Remove from heat; stir
to blend. Add sugar and eggs
to chocolate mixture; stir to
blend. Add flour mixture; stir
until just incorporated. Add the vanilla
and 1 cup of the chopped nuts. Spread batter evenly in a greased 9
by 13-inch pan, sprinkle with remaining ½ cup chopped nuts on top.
Bake at 350 degrees for 20-25 minutes.

Variation: *Use instead macadamia nuts, pecans.*

Hot Date with Chocolate

YIELD: 9 BY 13-INCH PAN

Sometimes, a clever recipe title is just a ruse, a trick to get the cook interested. But in this case, the title is both clever and accurate. Though it's quick and easy to make, these bars employ dates for subdued sweetness and moisture. They are positively gooey with chocolate. And they are really at their best when served fresh from the oven.

1 cup dates, chopped
1½ cups boiling water
1 teaspoon baking soda
½ cup butter, 1 stick
1 cup sugar
2 eggs, slightly beaten
1½ cup flour
½ teaspoon salt
¾ teaspoon baking soda
½ teaspoon baking powder
1 (16-ounce) package chocolate chips
¼ cup sugar
1 cup walnuts, chopped

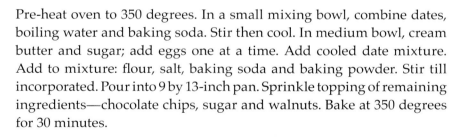

Pre-heat oven to 350 degrees. In a small mixing bowl, combine dates, boiling water and baking soda. Stir then cool. In medium bowl, cream butter and sugar; add eggs one at a time. Add cooled date mixture. Add to mixture: flour, salt, baking soda and baking powder. Stir till incorporated. Pour into 9 by 13-inch pan. Sprinkle topping of remaining ingredients—chocolate chips, sugar and walnuts. Bake at 350 degrees for 30 minutes.

Variation: *Try with macadamia nuts, pecans.*

It's a Fruit Cake Bar

Fruitcakes get a bad rap but this easy, crisp bar cookie will reintroduce you to candied fruits in a more than painless way. And you can choose just which ones you use, so if you hate those sugary cherries, leave 'em out; your mom's not looking!

For the crust:
2 cups all-purpose flour
½ cup sifted powdered sugar
1 cup unsalted butter (2 sticks), chilled and diced

For the topping:
½ cup all-purpose flour
1 teaspoon baking powder
⅓ teaspoon salt
1⅓ cups sugar
4 eggs
1 cup candied fruit, chopped
1 cup walnuts, chopped

Preheat oven to 350 degrees. Combine flour and sugar; cut in butter cubes. Press into greased pan. Bake at 350 degrees for 10 minutes

Meanwhile, sift flour, baking powder, salt and sugar into a bowl. Beat eggs and add to dry ingredients. Fold in fruits and nuts. Pour batter over baked crust. Bake at 350 degrees for 30-40 minutes. Cut while still warm and sprinkle with powdered sugar.

Variations: *Add candied citrus — lime, lemon, citron, orange, tangerine or pomelo.*

Chilly Pear Dessert

Don't scrimp on this cheese-cakey dessert: Buy the name brand (you know the one). And if you find really fresh, ripe but not mushy pears, use them instead of canned. You might also try slices of crisp, juicy Asian pears, but peel them first as their skins can be rather hard and bark-like.

For the crust:
    ½ cup unsalted butter, 1 stick
    ⅓ cup sugar
    ¼ teaspoon vanilla extract
    ¾ cup all-purpose flour
    ⅔ cup macadamia nuts, chopped (optional)

For the filling:
    8 ounces cream cheese
    ¼ cup sugar
    1 egg
    ½ teaspoon vanilla extract
    1 (28-ounce) can pears, drained and sliced

    1 teaspoon sugar
    1 teaspoon cinnamon

Prepare crust: Preheat oven to 350 degrees; grease or oil-spray 8 by 8-inch baking pan. In a mixing bowl, cream butter and sugar; add vanilla, flour and nuts. Press into greased pan and bake 10 minutes in a 350-degree oven.

Make filling: Combine cream cheese, sugar, egg and vanilla; beat until smooth. Refrigerate 15 minutes. Spread over baked crust.

Assemble: Arrange sliced pears over cream cheese mixture evenly. Combine sugar and cinnamon, then sprinkle over the pears. Bake at 375 degrees for 25 minutes and chill before serving.

Variation: *Add ½ cup cranberries.*

Pineapple
Butter Sponge Bars

There was a time when everything Hawaiian contained pineapple, or so it seemed; when Dole and Del Monte ruled the highlands. Still, canned pineapple is convenient and has earned its place beside fresh for uses such as this airy bar. (For one thing, canned pineapple has a consistent sweetness; today's fresh pineapple varies greatly in acid content depending on source and variety.)

½ cup butter (1 stick), melted and cooled
4 eggs, beaten
2 cups sugar
1½ cups cake flour
1 teaspoon baking powder
½ teaspoon baking soda
⅛ teaspoon salt
20 ounces crushed pineapple, well-drained
1 cup chopped nuts

Preheat oven to 350 degrees. Beat eggs and sugar until thick. Add dry ingredients, do not over-mix. Add cooled melted butter, drained pineapple and chopped nuts. Spread in shallow pan. Bake at 350 degrees for 25 minutes. Sprinkle with powdered sugar, and cut bars when cake is still warm.

Temptin' Rugelach

YIELD: 4 DOZEN COOKIES

Rugelach. Say it with a bit of catarrh in the throat: ROO-guh-leckchch. It means "royal" in Yiddish and these crescent-shaped pastries made with soft cream cheese dough explain why they're fit for royalty. Many, many varieties are made in Jewish households and bakeries, filled with jam, nuts, almond paste, dried fruit and more.

For the crust:
- 8 ounces cream cheese, room temperature
- 1 cup unsalted butter (2 sticks), room temperature
- ¼ cup sugar
- ¼ teaspoon salt
- 1 teaspoon vanilla extract
- 2 cups all-purpose flour

For the filling:
- 6 tablespoons sugar
- ¼ cup light brown sugar, packed
- ½ teaspoon cinnamon
- ¾ cup golden raisins
- 1 cup walnuts, chopped
- ½ cup raspberry jam (seedless)

To finish:
- 1 egg (beaten with 1 tablespoon water to make egg wash)
- 1 teaspoon cinnamon
- 3 tablespoons sugar

Make the crust: Cream the cream cheese and butter until light. Add ¼ cup sugar, salt and vanilla. Slowly mix in flour until just combined. Place dough on floured board and roll into a ball. Divide ball into four pieces, wrap each in plastic and refrigerate for 1 hour.

Make the filling: Combine 6 tablespoons sugar, brown sugar, ½ teaspoon cinnamon, raisins and nuts.

On well-floured board roll each ball of crust dough into a 9-inch circle. Spread dough with 2 tablespoons of jam and sprinkle with one-half cup of the filling. Lightly press filling into dough. Cut circle into 12 even wedges; first cut in quarters, then cut each quarter into thirds. Starting with wide edge, roll up towards the point. Place cookies, points tucked under, on a parchment-lined baking sheet. Chill 20 minutes.

Brush each cookie with egg wash. Combine 1 teaspoon cinnamon and 3 tablespoons sugar and sprinkle over cookies. Bake at 350 degrees for 15-20 minutes until lightly brown; cool on wire rack.

Variations: *Fill with macadamia nuts, chocolate, marzipan, poppy seed paste, or fruit preserves.*

Pumpkin Haupia Squares

YIELD: 9 BY 13-INCH PAN

Whoever came up with the idea of layering haupia and something else in a pie, thankyouthankyouthankyou! Here's one to try at holiday time, especially if your family isn't so hot about pumpkin (or you have a leftover can from conventional pumpkin pie-making).

For the crust:
- 2 cups all-purpose flour
- ⅔ cup powdered sugar
- 1 cup unsalted butter (2 sticks), chilled and cubed
- ½ cup chopped nuts

For the pumpkin layer:
- 15 ounces pumpkin purée
- 1 cup sugar
- ½ teaspoon vanilla extract
- ½ teaspoon cinnamon
- ½ teaspoon nutmeg
- ¼ teaspoon salt
- 12 ounces evaporated milk
- 2 eggs, beaten

For the haupia layer:
- ¼ cup sugar
- 6-7 tablespoons cornstarch
- ¼ cup water
- ½ cup milk
- 12 ounces frozen coconut milk, thawed

Grease a 9 by 13-inch pan and preheat oven to 350 degrees.

Make crust: Process flour and sugar with steel blade until thoroughly mixed. Add chilled butter cubes and nuts to mixture. Pulse until mixture is grainy. Press in prepared pan. Bake at 350 degrees for 15-20 minutes.

Make pumpkin layer: Hand-mix all ingredients together until combined. Pour over baked crust. Bake at 350 degrees for 30-35 minutes; cool.

Make haupia layer: Combine sugar, milk and coconut milk in saucepan, bring to a simmer. Combine water and cornstarch to make a slurry. Slowly add to simmering milk mixture. Bring to a boil and cook until thickened. Allow to cool slightly and pour over baked pumpkin layer; smooth top.

Chill pie till haupia is firm.

charming
cupcakes & cakes

Let us eat cake. Please. While made-from-scratch cakes have grown scarce in home kitchens, the appearance of such a cake (or its little sister, the cupcake, now enjoying a Renaissance) still signals something special.

Remember that a made-from-scratch cake won't include the many life-extending chemicals used by commercial bakers; it's meant to be eaten the day it's made, preferably while the frosting-crusted beaters are still in the sink!

Don't throw dry cake crumbs away: Use as a topping or in a crumb pie crust. Or make a steamed pudding by combining cake crumbs with softened butter, your preferred jam, chopped nuts and a beaten egg; then placing in a buttered mold and steaming on a rack until firm—an old-fashioned treat little known today.

Cinnamon Apple Cake

Dig out that old spring form pan from the last time you made a baked cheesecake or quiche and try this homey yet sophisticated number with the flavor of fall in fresh apples and ground cinnamon.

For the topping:
 ¼ cup light brown sugar
 1 teaspoon cinnamon
 3 tablespoons unsalted butter, melted

For the cake:
 ½ cup all-purpose flour
 ⅓ cup sugar
 1 tablespoon baking powder
 1 teaspoon cinnamon
 ⅛ teaspoon salt
 ½ teaspoon vanilla extract
 2 eggs, beaten
 2 tablespoons unsalted butter, melted
 ⅓ cup milk
 4 cups apple slices, peeled and cored (approximately 4 apples)

Make the topping: Combine sugar, cinnamon and melted butter. Set aside.

Make the cake: Preheat oven to 400 degrees. In a medium bowl, combine flour, sugar, baking powder, cinnamon and salt; set aside. In a small bowl, mix vanilla extract, eggs, melted butter and milk. Add wet ingredients to dry ingredients; stir until blended. Add apple slices and coat with batter. Pour batter into greased 9-inch spring form pan and bake at 400 degrees until slightly firm and golden, about 25 minutes. Remove pan from oven and sprinkle topping over cake. Return to oven and bake until top is golden or when tested in the center with a toothpick, comes out clean, about another 10 minutes. Place cake on wire rack to cool. Run a knife around sides of pan and release and remove spring form side; leave cake on base of pan. Serve at room temperature.

Easy Chocolate Coffee Mug Cake

YIELD: 2 SERVINGS (PER MUG)

Oh, this is too cute for words: "Bake" a cake in a microwavable coffee mug and share it with someone special. But watch out! When it emerges from the oven, this is one hot mama! You'll need one (8-10 ounce) microwavable coffee mug.

4 tablespoons all-purpose flour
4 tablespoons sugar
2 tablespoons unsweetened cocoa powder
1 egg
3 tablespoons milk
3 tablespoons vegetable oil
⅛ teaspoon vanilla extract
3 tablespoons semi-sweet chocolate chips

Place dry ingredients in coffee mug and mix well. Add egg and mix thoroughly. Pour in milk and oil; mix well. Add chocolate chips; mix in. Place coffee mug in microwave for 3 minutes (in a 1,000-watt oven; adjust for more or less powerful ovens).

Note: Cake may rise over the top of mug, allow to cool before eating.

Variations: *Add ¼ teaspoon grated orange rind or ⅛ teaspoon flavoring of your choice — cherry, mint, raspberry, or coffee extracts.*

Piña Colada Pound Cake

If you like Piña Coladas . . . sorry, couldn't resist. Here's a pound cake that tastes like the ultimate lounge lizard drink, with coconut and a splash of pineapple. You'll be discoing at first bite.

1½ cups all-purpose flour
1½ cups cake flour
¼ teaspoon salt
1 cup butter, softened
2½ cups sugar
4 eggs, room temperature
½ teaspoon pure lemon extract
½ teaspoon vanilla extract
6 ounces sour cream
3 tablespoons unsweetened coconut milk
¾ cup shredded coconut

For the pineapple glaze:
½ cup pineapple juice
1 tablespoon fresh Meyer lemon juice
⅔ cup sugar

Grease and flour two loaf pans. Preheat oven to 350 degrees. Sift flours and salt; set aside. Beat butter and sugar until light and creamy. Add eggs one at a time. Add lemon and vanilla extracts; mix well. Alternately mix in dry ingredients and sour cream, starting with dry and ending with dry ingredients. Reduce speed and slowly incorporate coconut milk and coconut flakes. Divide batter evenly in loaf pans. Bake at 350 degrees for 1¼ hours. To test doneness, insert toothpick to the middle of cake. If it comes out clean, it's done. Transfer to wire rack and cool cake in pan for 30 minutes. Invert warm cakes on parchment paper over rack.

While the cake bakes, making pineapple glaze: Heat water, juice, and sugar over low heat until sugar dissolves. Strain mixture. Brush warm cake(s) with the glaze. Allow cake(s) to cool before serving.

Variation: *Use a Bundt cake mold, spreading batter evenly. Bake for 1¼ hours.*

German Chocolate Cake

German Chocolate Cakes — from a mix — became all the rage in the 1960s and what's not to like about this confection, credited to an American named Sam German? Chocolate, a sort of Chantilly cream studded with coconuts and pecans? Can't find a thing.

For the cake:
- 4 ounces semi-sweet baking chocolate bar
- 2¼ cups sifted cake flour
- 1½ cups sugar
- 1 teaspoon baking soda
- ½ teaspoon baking powder
- ½ teaspoon salt
- ⅔ cups unsalted butter
- 1 cup buttermilk
- 1 teaspoon vanilla extract
- 2 eggs

For the frosting:
- 1 cup evaporated milk
- 1 cup sugar
- 3 egg yolks, slightly beaten
- ½ cup unsalted butter
- 1 teaspoon vanilla extract
- 1¼ cups sweetened coconut flakes
- 1 cup chopped pecans

Make the cake: Preheat oven to 350 degrees. Melt chocolate; cool. Sift together flour, sugar, baking soda, baking powder and salt. Cream butter in mixing bowl; add flour mixture, ¾ cup buttermilk and vanilla. Beat 2 minutes at medium speed. Add melted chocolate, eggs and ¼ cup buttermilk; beat 1 minute. Pour batter into three 8-inch greased cake pans lined with parchment paper on bottom. Bake 350 degrees for 15-20 minutes, until toothpick inserted in center comes out clean. Cool in pans 15 minutes; remove cake from pans onto wire racks, cool completely before frosting cakes. Spread frosting on layers and stack.

Make frosting while cake is baking: Combine milk, sugar, egg yolks, butter and vanilla in saucepan. Cook and stir over medium heat until thickens, about 12 minutes. Remove from heat. Add coconut and pecans. Cool to spreading consistency, stirring occasionally.

Pucker Up, Prune Apple Cake

YIELD: 10-12 SLICES

Prune cake was a lū'au standard in the Islands in the mid-20th century. This lighter-than-usual contemporary version makes use of stewed prunes preserved with li hing powder (homemade or buy it at shops that sell local-style "crack seed" snacks).

2 cups sugar
1½ cups vegetable oil
3 eggs
3 cups all-purpose flour
2 teaspoons baking soda
1 teaspoon salt
1 teaspoon cinnamon
½ teaspoon nutmeg
12 ounces pitted li hing prunes (chopped, about 2 cups)
2 cups coarsely shredded apples
1 cup chopped nuts
Powdered sugar for dusting

Butter and flour a 10-inch tube pan or bundt cake pan, or treat with oil-flour spray. Preheat oven to 325 degrees. In a standing mixer or a large bowl with a hand-held mixer beat together sugar, oil and eggs at medium speed about 2 minutes. Sift together flour, baking soda, salt, cinnamon and nutmeg. Slowly add dry ingredients to egg mixture. Add prunes, apples and nuts at low speed; blend thoroughly. Spread batter in prepared pan. Bake at 325 degrees for 1½ hours or until toothpick emerges clean from center. Cool in pan 15 minutes, then invert onto wire rack to cool completely, and dust with powdered sugar.

Variations:

- *Use mini-bundt pans and bake 30 minutes.*
- *Choose walnuts, pecans or a mixture of the two.*

Mango Upside Down Cake

Upside-down cakes began as stovetop "skillet cakes," baked in a well-seasoned black cast iron pan. First, the cook melted butter and sugar to make a caramel; fresh or dried fruit would be arranged on this and topped with a buttery batter. Once baked, the cake would be turned out on its head. Here's a version to use in mango season, made in individual portions.

For the cake:
- **4 cups all-purpose flour**
- **6 tablespoons semolina flour**
- **1 tablespoon baking powder**
- **1 teaspoon salt**
- **⅔ cup butter**
- **1½ cups sugar**
- **8 eggs, separated**
- **1 tablespoon vanilla extract**
- **1⅓ cups milk**
- **½ cup sugar**

For the topping:
- **1 cup butter**
- **2½ cups brown sugar**
- **2 cups mango, peeled and cubed**

Preheat oven to 350 degrees. Grease muffin molds (two tins of 12 each). In a medium bowl, whisk together dry ingredients; set aside. In a large bowl, cream together butter and sugar until light-colored and fluffy. Gently mix in 8 egg yolks, one at a time. Add vanilla extract. Be sure the wet mixture is homogenous and smooth; then alternately beat in dry ingredients and milk. In a separate medium, clean, dry bowl, whip 8 egg whites and sugar to firm peaks. Gently fold whipped whites into batter. In a small saucepan, melt butter and stir in brown sugar; cook, stirring, until sugar is dissolved (do not allow to boil or it will candy). Remove from heat.

To assemble cakes: Place a tablespoon of topping and 3-4 pieces of cubed mango in the bottom of each greased muffin mold. Fill molds to within ½ inch of top with cake batter. Bake at 350 degrees for 12-15 minutes until toothpick emerges clean.

Guava Marbled Cheesecake

If you're paying for guavas, you're not paying attention to the laden trees you probably pass whenever you drive into the country in the fall. Here, tart, intense guava juice (make your own or buy frozen concentrate) is swirled through a rich baked cheese.

For the glaze:
- 2½ cups guava juice
- 1 cup sugar
- 1 tablespoon cornstarch whisked into ⅓ cup water

For the cheesecake:
- 2 prepared graham cracker pie crusts
- 2 (8-ounce) packages cream cheese, softened
- 3 eggs
- 1 can sweetened condensed milk
- 2 teaspoons vanilla extract

Preheat oven to 350 degrees. In a small saucepan, heat guava juice and sugar to simmering. Whisk in cornstarch mixture a little at a time to the guava mixture until the glaze coats the back of the spoon; cool and reserve.

Using a stand or hand-held mixer, cream together cream cheese, sweetened condensed milk and vanilla till incorporated. Add eggs one at a time, mixing on low speed. Divide mixture evenly between the two pie crusts. Drizzle all but ½ cup of the guava glaze over the cakes in puddles, then swirl through the cream cheese mixture with a knife or chopstick. Bake at 350 degrees for 50 minutes, until a knife emerges clean from the center. Cool on rack 1 hour, and then glaze with remaining guava juice mixture. Chill 30 minutes before serving.

Got Coffee Cake?

YIELD: 24 PIECES

Coffee cake has gotten a bit lost amidst today's cupcakes and energy bars, but it's an easy option that goes together quickly. Coffee actually brings out the flavors of buttery, spiced baked goods.

<u>*For the cake:*</u>
   2 cups all-purpose flour
   1 teaspoon baking powder
   1 teaspoon baking soda
   ½ teaspoon salt
   1 cup unsalted butter, 2 sticks
   1 cup sugar
   2 eggs
   1 teaspoon vanilla extract
   8 ounces sour cream

<u>*For the topping:*</u>
   3 tablespoons brown sugar
   ½ cup chopped nuts
   1 teaspoon cinnamon

Preheat oven to 350 degrees. Butter and flour or oil-and-flour spray a 9 by 13-inch baking pan. In a medium bowl, sift together flour, baking powder, baking soda and salt; set aside. In a large bowl, cream butter, sugar, eggs, vanilla and sour cream. Stir in dry ingredients until combined. In a small bowl, combine topping ingredients. Spread half the batter in the prepared pan; sprinkle half the topping; repeat. Bake at 350 degrees for 30-35 minutes.

Variations: *Try walnuts or macadamia nuts.*

Tiramisu

YIELD: 12-16 PIECES

The dessert of the 1980s, tiramisu (teer-ah-mee-SUE), is generally made with coffee-soaked ladyfingers. Here, the coffee is omitted for a crispier texture. Keep dessert chilled up to serving time. Since this dish is uncooked, be sure to use pasteurized eggs for safety.

3 egg yolks
3 tablespoons powdered sugar
8 ounces mascarpone cheese, softened
3 egg whites
3 tablespoons sugar
2 ounces semi-sweet chocolate bar, grated
1 cup whipping cream
3 tablespoons powdered sugar
12 ladyfingers, split

Chill a medium bowl for later use. In another medium bowl, using a hand-held mixer, beat egg yolks with powdered sugar until pale yellow. Blend in mascarpone; mix until smooth. In a separate bowl with clean beaters, beat egg whites with sugar until stiff. Fold egg whites into cheese mixture. In the chilled bowl, beat whipping cream and powdered sugar to soft peaks; set aside.

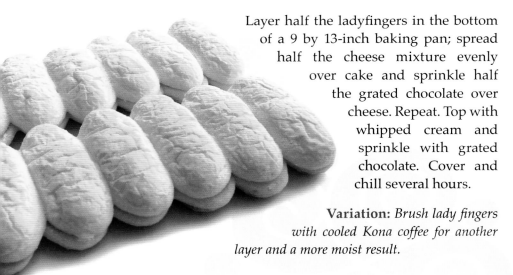

Layer half the ladyfingers in the bottom of a 9 by 13-inch baking pan; spread half the cheese mixture evenly over cake and sprinkle half the grated chocolate over cheese. Repeat. Top with whipped cream and sprinkle with grated chocolate. Cover and chill several hours.

Variation: *Brush lady fingers with cooled Kona coffee for another layer and a more moist result.*

Kalamansi Cupcakes

YIELD: ABOUT 24 CUPCAKES

Kalamansi, Philippines lime, is a very tart citrus fruit, small and green-to-bright orange in color; it's a lime-tangerine cross. These cupcakes are frosted with a one-time kitchen staple: 7-Minute Meringue Icing.

<u>For the cupcakes:</u>
- **1 cup butter, softened**
- **2 cups sugar**
- **3 eggs**
- **2 teaspoons kalamansi zest**
- **1 teaspoon vanilla extract**
- **3½ cups all-purpose OR cake flour OR 1¼ cups of each**
- **1 teaspoon baking soda**
- **½ teaspoon baking powder**
- **½ teaspoon salt**
- **2 cups sour cream**
- **Kalamansi 7-Minute Meringue Icing (recipe on page 70)**

Preheat oven to 350 degrees. In a stand mixer or using a hand-held mixer, cream together butter and sugar until light-colored and fluffy. Beat in eggs one at a time. Stir in kalamansi zest and vanilla and mix well. In a medium bowl, whisk together flour, baking soda, baking powder and salt. Add dry mixture to creamed mixture alternately with sour cream. Batter will be thick. Insert cupcake liners and fill with ¼ cup batter. Bake at 350 degrees for 12-17 minutes or until a toothpick emerges clean from center. Cool on rack.

Frost with 7-Minute Meringue Icing.

Kalamansi 7-Minute Meringue Icing

YIELD: 3 CUPS

6-8 kalamansi
3 large egg whites
1½ cups sugar
Pinch salt
3 tablespoons water
1 tablespoon light corn syrup
¼ teaspoon cream of tartar

Zest and then juice the kalamansi to make 3 tablespoons of juice (strain away seeds), ½ teaspoon zest; set aside. In the top of a large double boiler (or a heatproof bowl), combine kalamansi juice, egg whites, sugar, salt, water, corn syrup and cream of tartar. Beat until thoroughly blended. Set over boiling water, which is not touching the bowl; beat constantly with a hand-held mixer at medium-high speed or with a wire whisk, until the mixture stands in stiff peaks, about 7-10 minutes. Remove from heat and continue beating until the icing is cooled to room temperature. Add the kalamansi zest at this point and blend until combined.

Peter, Peter, Pumpkin Cake

YIELD: 24 PIECES

Here's another use for pumpkin pie filling (the kind that is already spiced) — an easy cake. Or try using fresh kabocha pumpkin, which has a lovely silky texture and delicate flavor. Microwave, bake or steam a couple of the small, green-skinned pumpkins until readily pierced with a fork; halve the pumpkins, scrape out seeds, cut flesh out and mash to make 3 cups, then spice as desired.

3 cups all-purpose flour
1 cup vegetable oil
½ cup butter (1 stick), melted
3 cups canned pumpkin pie filling
3 cups sugar
2 teaspoons baking soda
1½ teaspoons baking powder
1 teaspoon cinnamon
6 eggs

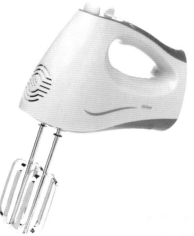

Preheat oven to 350 degrees. Oil-spray a 9 by 13-inch baking pan. In a large bowl, beat together all ingredients, mixing well until combined. Pour batter into prepared pan, spreading evenly.

Bake at 350 degrees for 45 minutes.

Red Velvet Cupcakes

YIELD: 24 CUPCAKES

"She-e wore red ve-el-vet!" Seems like everybody is making old-fashioned red velvet cupcakes these days. Visit a craft store or kitchen supply shop or go online to find food-safe red gel paste for the truest color.

2½ cups cake flour
½ cup cocoa powder
1 teaspoon baking soda
½ teaspoon salt
1 cup butter, softened
2 cups sugar
4 eggs
1 cup sour cream
½ cup milk
1 tablespoon gel paste red food color or 2 tablespoons liquid
    food coloring
2 teaspoons vanilla extract
Butter frosting (recipe on page 74)

Preheat oven to 350 degrees. Place fluted liners in cupcake pans. In a medium bowl, sift together flour, cocoa powder, baking soda and salt; set aside. In a stand mixer or a large bowl with a hand-held mixer, cream together butter and sugar until light-colored and fluffy. Beat in eggs one at a time. Stir in sour cream, milk, food coloring and vanilla. Gradually beat in flour mixture on low speed until just incorporated. Do not overbeat. Fill cups two-thirds full. Bake at 350 degrees for 12-17 minutes or until toothpick emerges clean.

Butter Frosting

YIELD: 3 CUPS

This classic is the frosting many will remember from the days before cakes came from boxes and were topped with stuff that came from cans. It's readily flavored as you wish, with different extracts, with coconut milk instead of dairy milk, with the addition of such ingredients as angel-flake coconut or chopped nuts. Unless you have a climate-controlled home, do not attempt to make this on a hot, humid day; it will literally melt into the cake!

1 pound unsalted butter (4 sticks), softened
2 pounds powdered sugar
⅛ teaspoon salt
2 tablespoons vanilla extract
2 tablespoons milk

In a large mixing bowl or stand mixer with paddle attachment, combine all ingredients and mix on low until sugar is moistened.

Increase speed to medium-high and beat until creamy and fluffy, for about 1½ minutes, scraping down bowl and paddle twice to make sure all ingredients are mixed evenly. Do not over-whip or frosting will be too soft for piping. Frost cooled cakes; if frosting is held, do so in an airtight container in the refrigerator.

Mango Cake

Oh, for the days when nobody had to buy mangoes; they just appeared on your porch! When you get some good, fresh, local mango, try this cake, lighter than familiar mango bread, and more sophisticated.

Mixture 1:
- 3 eggs, slightly beaten
- 1 teaspoon vanilla extract
- 1 cup vegetable oil
- 2 cups mashed mango
- ½ cup sweetened shredded coconut
- ½ cup golden raisins
- ¼ cup chopped walnuts

Mixture 2:
- 2 cups all-purpose flour
- 2 teaspoons cinnamon
- 2 teaspoons baking soda
- 1 teaspoon baking powder
- ½ teaspoon salt
- 1½ cups sugar

Topping:
- ⅔ cup crushed cornflakes
- ¼ cup chopped nuts
- ¼ cup light brown sugar
- 2 tablespoons melted butter

Butter or oil-spray a 9 by 13-inch baking pan. Preheat oven to 350 degrees. In a medium bowl, combine Mixture 1 ingredients. Do the same with Mixture 2. In a large bowl, combine the two and let stand 20 minutes. Spread this batter in prepared pan. In a small bowl, mix topping ingredients and sprinkle over batter.

Bake at 350 degrees for 45 minutes.

Black Forest Chocolate Cupcakes

YIELD: 24 CUPCAKES

Black Forest Cake is a classic, flavored with Kirschwasser, a tart cherry liqueur made in the Schwarzwalder ("black forest"), southern Germany. By German law, no cake can be called a Black Forest Cake unless it contains a certain percentage of the liqueur. Cherry flavors this chocolate cupcake from to bottom, with whole cherries inside and on top and a fluffy liqueur-spiked frosting.

2⅔ cup all-purpose flour
½ teaspoon baking soda
4 teaspoons baking powder
1½ cups cocoa powder
¼ teaspoon salt
3 ounces butter, softened
3 cups sugar
4 eggs
1½ teaspoons vanilla extract
2 cups milk
1 (21-ounce) can cherry pie filling (strain sauce and reserve)
1 plain milk chocolate candy bar (i.e. Hershey's); refrigerated
1 small bottle maraschino cherries, drained
  OR 24 whole cherries
Fluffy Kirschwasser Frosting (recipe on page 78)

Preheat oven to 350 degrees. Insert fluted cupcake liners. In a medium bowl, sift together flour, baking soda, baking powder, cocoa powder and salt; set aside. In a stand mixer or medium bowl with hand-held mixer, cream together butter and sugar until light-colored and fluffy. Beat in eggs one at a time. Stir in vanilla extract and reserved cherry filling sauce. Add flour mixture alternately with milk; beat well. Fill lined cupcake pans three-quarter full. Place a cherry or two in each. Bake at 350 degrees for 12-15 minutes or until toothpick emerges clean. Cool on rack. Frost with Fluffy Kirschwasser Frosting. Decorate with chocolate shavings (use a vegetable peeler on the refrigerated chocolate bar) and a fresh Bing cherry (in season) or drained maraschino cherries.

Fluffy
Kirschwasser Frosting

YIELD: 3 CUPS

3 large egg whites
1½ cups sugar
Pinch salt
2 tablespoons water
4 tablespoons Kirschwasser (cherry liqueur)
1 tablespoon light corn syrup
¼ teaspoon cream of tartar

Combine all ingredients in the top of a large double boiler or a heatproof bowl and beat until thoroughly blended. Set over boiling water, which is not touching the bowl. Beat constantly with a hand-held mixer at medium-high speed or with a wire whisk, until the mixture stands in stiff peaks, approximately for 7 minutes. Remove from heat and continue beating until the icing is cooled to room temperature.

pies, tarts & tartlets

A pie is defined as a pastry filled with sliced, chopped or ground ingredients — sweet (fruits, nuts, custards) or savory (meats, fish, eggs or cheese). The earliest pies were savory, hearty mixtures baked in brick or masonry ovens with the crust serving as the plate. In Colonia America, apple pie was survival food: Apples aged well in the root cellar, any off flavor masked by spices (though sugar was too precious to use in quantity); crust was made with meat drippings. Delicate, multi-layered pastry, rich in butter and sugar came later, with wealth. Today, things are a bit more mixed up: You can find rustic, hand-rolled pies in white-tablecloth restaurants and puff pastry turnovers in convenience stores.

Simple Pie Crust

YIELD: 1 (9-INCH) PIE CRUST

If you can master pie crust, you're three-quarters of the way there. The tricks: use iced water (place ice cubes in water and measure when very cold) and work quickly. And don't let anybody tell you that really flaky, light pastry can be made with oil; chilled solid shortening or butter is a must.

1½ cups all-purpose flour
½ teaspoon salt
½ teaspoon sugar
½ cup shortening
3 tablespoons cold water
   (place ice cubes in cup and add water)

In a small bowl, whisk together flour, salt and sugar. Cut in shortening with pastry cutter or two knives. Sprinkle ice water over dough 1 tablespoon at a time, until dough pulls together and is easy to handle. Working lightly and quickly, flatten dough into a round disc. Cover with plastic wrap and chill for at least an hour. Roll out on floured surface to about ¼-inch thick and about 1 inch larger than the diameter of the pie pan. Preheat oven to 400 degrees. To bake the crust "blind" for uncooked fillings, line the pie plate with crust, pierce in several places with the tines of a fork. Line crust with raw beans or pie crust fillers and bake at 400 degrees for 10-12 minutes until golden-brown.

A is for Apple Pie

This modern-day sweet apple pie is best made with a mixture of tart "cooking" apples, such as Braeburn or Granny Smith, and a sweeter apple such as Fuji or Gala. For an interesting twist, substitute Chinese 5-Spice for the cinnamon or use pumpkin pie spice, which includes nutmeg and clove, instead of plain cinnamon.

2 (9-inch) Simple Pie Crust (recipe on page 80), do not bake, keep rolled out

For the filling:
7 apples
¾ cup sugar
2 tablespoons all-purpose flour
¾ teaspoon ground cinnamon
2 tablespoons chilled butter, diced
1 tablespoon milk
1 tablespoon sugar for dusting top of pie

Preheat oven to 375 degrees. Peel, core and thinly slice apples; place in a mixing bowl and toss with sugar, flour and cinnamon. Arrange apple slices evenly in pastry-lined pie pan. Dot fruit with diced butter. Cover apples with second crust and flute edges. Cut slit into top of pie so steam can escape. Brush top of pie with milk then sprinkle with sugar. Place pie pan on lined baking sheet to catch any spillover from pie filling. Bake at 375-400 degrees for 50 minutes.

Custard Pie

A great custard pie is creamy with a crisp crust. To keep the crust from getting soggy, use a perforated pie pan or prick holes in a disposable aluminum pie pan (poke from the inside out). The holes will provide air flow.

1 (9-inch) Simple Pie Crust (recipe on page 80), do not bake, keep rolled out and lining pie pan

For the filling:
4 eggs, room temperature
½ cup sugar
¼ teaspoon salt
2 teaspoons vanilla extract
2½ cups milk
1 pinch nutmeg (optional)

Preheat oven to 400 degrees. In a medium bowl, combine eggs, sugar, salt and vanilla extract, stirring well. Add milk; skim off any foam. Pour custard through a sieve into prepared pie pan. Sprinkle nutmeg over the top. Carefully place pie onto a baking pan, then into oven and bake at 400 degrees for 15 minutes; reduce heat to 350 degrees and bake for another 15-20 minutes until the jiggly texture of soft Jell-O. Do not over-bake. A knife in the center should emerge clean.

Guava Frangipane Tartlets

Frangipane, a tart lined with almond paste, is an haute cuisine classic with a subtle, sophisticated flavor. The paste not only yields sweet flavor, it helps prevent juices from seeping into the crust. Here, it's made in miniature, with a tropical flair. You can use muffin tins if you don't want to invest in mini-tart pans.

For the crust:
- 1¼ cups all-purpose flour
- ½ cup powdered sugar
- ¾ cup unsalted butter, diced, chilled
- 2 egg yolks, beaten (save the egg white for filling)
- 1 tablespoon water

For the filling:
- ½ cup unsalted butter
- ⅓ cup almond paste
- ½ cup sugar
- 3 eggs, lightly beaten plus 1 egg white (from crust)
- ½ cup cake flour
- 1 cup guava jam

Powdered sugar for serving

Make the crust: In food processor combine flour and sugar; pulse to combine. Add butter and pulse until pea-size crumbs form. While pulsing, add beaten egg yolks and process to form moist crumbs.

Place dough on floured surface and shaped into a flat disc, divide in half. Wrap each in plastic wrap and refrigerate for at least one hour.

Roll out chilled dough to ⅛-inch thickness. Using a 3-inch round cutter, cut out 12 rounds of pastry. Press each round into greased mini tart pans or greased mini muffin pans. Using your fingers press crust to fit into the well. Repeat process with second batch of dough. Refrigerate until ready to use.

recipe continued on page 86

Make the filling: In a food processor, beat butter until light and creamy. Add the almond paste and sugar; beat until smooth. Continue adding eggs one at a time, then add one egg white from the crust recipe. Reduce speed and gently fold in cake flour until just blended.

Assemble: Preheat oven to 400 degrees. Spoon about 1 tablespoon of jam into bottom of each tart shell, making a thin layer on the bottom. Spoon filling over the jam, till about one-quarter from the top of the tart shell. Bake at 400 degrees for 12-15 minutes until golden. Cool on wire racks. Dust with powdered sugar before serving.

Variations: *Use instead, strawberry, poha or pineapple jam.*

Apple Frangipane Tart

YIELD: 1 (10-INCH) TART PAN

Here's another frangipane, more typical of what you'd learn in a traditional French baking class, made with apples and baked in a large tart pan. A tart pan is a shallow metal round, generally fluted, with a bottom and rim that separate. Once the tart is baked and cooled, the rim slips off and the bottom remains to support the tart.

1 (9-inch) Simple Pie Crust (recipe on page 80), do not bake
1 cup sliced almonds
2 tablespoons all-purpose flour
½ cup sugar
½ cup unsalted butter
2 teaspoons almond extract
1 egg, room temperature
¼ teaspoon salt
2 apples, peeled, cored and sliced
2 tablespoons apple jelly, melted

For the crust: Lightly butter 10-inch tart pan with removable rim. Roll dough out an inch larger than the pan diameter. Gently lay the pie crust inside the pan and lightly press into place. Trim off excess. Roll excess into a thin rope and press into the inside edges of the pan to reinforce the tart; set aside (refrigerate if you have to hold it for any length of time).

For the filling: Lightly toast almonds on a baking pan at 300 degrees for 7 minutes or until golden and fragrant.

Preheat oven to 400 degrees. Place almonds in food processor with flour and sugar and process to a smooth paste. Add butter, almond extract, egg and salt and process until incorporated. Scoop paste evenly into the prepared tart shell. Place apples decoratively over paste. Brush apples with jelly. Bake at 400 degrees for 25-30 minutes, until pastry is puffed and golden brown.

Pumpkin Chiffon

The light, sweet, gelatin-filled concoction called Pumpkin Chiffon was invented by Monroe Boston Strause as an alternative to conventional pumpkin custard pie. Use canned solid pumpkin, not the spiced and sweetened pie filling.

1 (9-inch) Simple Pie Crust (recipe on page 80), baked and cooled

For the filling:
- **2 teaspoons gelatin**
- **¼ cup milk**
- **3 eggs (separated)**
- **½ cup light brown sugar**
- **1¼ cups canned pumpkin (not pumpkin pie filling)**
- **½ teaspoon salt**
- **½ teaspoon ground cinnamon**
- **¼ teaspoon ground nutmeg**
- **½ cup sugar**
- **½ cup milk**

Whipped cream

Dissolve gelatin in ¼ cup milk for 5 minutes. Set aside. In a medium saucepan, beat egg yolks, then add light brown sugar, pumpkin, salt, cinnamon and nutmeg. Cook over low heat, stirring constantly until mixture begins to thicken. Add gelatin to hot pumpkin mixture and stir until dissolves. Set aside and allow to cool. In a medium bowl, whip egg whites until almost stiff, beat in ½ cup sugar, 1 tablespoon at a time. Fold in beaten egg whites into cooled pumpkin mixture. Pour pumpkin mixture into pre-baked pie shell. Chill. Serve with whipped cream.

Haupia
Chocolate Cream Pie

YIELD: 1 (9-INCH) PIE

This is easy to make with a premade pie shell.
Bake and cool the shell and fill; chill further.

1 (9-inch) Simple Pie Crust (recipe on page 80),
   baked and cooled
1 large box instant chocolate pudding mix
3½ cups low fat milk
3 cups canned coconut milk
½ cup sugar
½ teaspoon salt
5 tablespoons butter
½ cup cornstarch
½ teaspoon vanilla extract
1 can whipped topping (or fresh whipped cream)

Preheat oven to 400 degrees. Bake pie shell "blind." Cool.

In a medium bowl, mix the chocolate pudding with the low fat milk chill in the refrigerator until set; set aside. In a medium saucepan, bring to a boil the coconut milk, sugar, salt, and butter. Dissolve cornstarch with a little water, then add to coconut mixture to thicken to pudding texture. Remove from heat; add vanilla extract. Pour coconut pudding into pie shell and let it cool at room temperature. Then spoon the chocolate pudding over the coconut pudding. Chill for 15 minutes or until firm. Serve with whipped cream.

freshbread

Many people feel they haven't eaten unless they've eaten bread; it is, indeed, the staff of life for Westerners, in the place of rice or noodles for other cultures. Bread baking bears a certain mystique but it's masterable if you're tolerant of a few failures. And quick breads are a snap. Whether it involves yeast or baking powder, people are always impressed when you present them with a fresh-baked loaf of bread and say, "I made it myself!"

In baking, it's important to read directions carefully, use the correct-sized pan, be sure yeast (if it's used) is still viable and don't tarry after you've added liquid to quick bread batters made with baking powder and/or baking soda.

Jungle Monkey Bread

Who doesn't love pull-apart sweet rolls?
Kids find the title Jungle Monkey Bread hilarious — plus they get to eat with their hands! This shortcut recipe uses prepared refrigerated biscuits.

1 can refrigerated buttermilk biscuits
½ cup unsalted butter, melted
½ - ¾ cup sugar
½ teaspoon ground cinnamon

Preheat oven to 375 degrees. In a small bowl, combine sugar and cinnamon. Cut each biscuit into fourths. Roll each piece in melted butter then in the sugar-cinnamon mixture. Place 3-4 pieces into each greased muffin cup. Bake at 375 degrees for 8-10 minutes, until puffed and golden brown.

Hot Potato Rolls

Potato lends moisture and a slight background richness to breads. This recipe for rolls is by far best when you start with a real, boiled potato, peeled and mashed, but you can "cheat" with instant mashed potatoes. For something different, try using herb- or garlic-flavored mashed potatoes.

**1 cup mashed potatoes (instant or made from 1 medium
  potato, peeled, cooked, mashed)**
2 packages yeast
½ cup warm water
⅔ cup shortening
⅔ cup sugar
1 teaspoon salt
1 cup scalded milk
2 eggs, beaten
7-8 cups all-purpose flour

Papaya Pineapple Fruit Butter (recipe on page 95)

Preheat oven to 350 degrees. Sprinkle yeast over warm water; stir to dissolve. Set aside for 3-5 minutes to "bloom." Combine shortening, sugar, salt, mashed potatoes and milk. Add yeast and mix together. Add eggs and combine. Add 7 cups of the flour to make a soft dough; use more flour if necessary. Grease large bowl with melted butter, then place dough into greased bowl; rub rest of melted butter roll top of dough. Cover tightly and place in refrigerator for at least 2-3 hours. Pinch off dough into desired shape and place on baking sheet. Allow dough to rise until double in size. Bake at 300 degrees for 15-20 minutes. Serve with Papaya Pineapple Fruit Butter.

Papaya Pineapple Fruit Butter

½ cup butter (1 stick), room temperature
1 tablespoon confectioners' sugar
1½ tablespoons Papaya Pineapple Jam

In a small container, mix together the butter, confectioners' sugar and Papaya Pineapple Jam until thoroughly combine. Chill & use generously.

Use only jams, marmalade, conserves (whole fruit jam) or fruit preserves which are free of liquid.

Variations: *Lilikoi Jam, Mango Jam, Poha Jam, Strawberry Fruit Preserves.*

Easy Beer Bread

*Don't think you're going to use up old beer on this beer bread;
you need some fizz to produce the air pockets that lighten the bread.
Use a darker beer for more molasses-type flavor.*

½ cup unsalted butter (1 stick)
1½ cups all-purpose flour
1 cup whole wheat flour
½ cup rolled oats
3 tablespoons sugar
1 tablespoon baking powder
½ teaspoon baking soda
1 teaspoon salt
1 (12 ounce) bottle good-quality beer (light or
   dark, but not stout, room temperature)

Place an oven rack in the upper third of the oven and preheat the oven to 350 degrees. Place butter in a 9 by 13 by 2-inch baking pan or dish and set it in the oven while oven is preheating.

Stir together flours, oats, sugar, baking powder, baking soda and salt in a medium size mixing bowl. Stir in the beer until it just incorporated. Dough will be sticky and heavy; set aside.

Remove baking pan from oven. Carefully pour 6 tablespoons of melted butter out of the pan into a cup. Tilt the pan to coat the bottom and sides with the remaining butter in the pan. Spoon the bread dough into the pan and spread evenly; drizzle the 6 tablespoons of melted butter over the top of the dough. Bake at 350 degrees for 20-25 minutes or until golden brown. Remove the bread from the oven to a cooling rack; cool. Cut into rectangles and serve warm.

Applesauce Bread

YIELD: 8 BY 4-INCH LOAF PAN

Applesauce is a favorite of bakers for a number of reasons: it adds both moisture and body to baked goods with a gentle sweetness that can be brought forward or placed in the background, depending on seasoning. The following recipe adds interest by mains of raisins, dried cranberries and nuts. It's also quite versatile; mashed pumpkin or squash or even grated zucchini could be substituted.

½ cup unsalted butter, room temperature
¼ cup light brown sugar
2 cups all-purpose flour
1 teaspoon baking powder
1 teaspoon baking soda
½ teaspoon salt
1 teaspoon cinnamon
1 teaspoon nutmeg
1 teaspoon vanilla extract
1¼ cups applesauce, bottled
2 eggs
½ cup golden raisins
½ cup dried cranberries
½ cup macadamia nuts, chopped

Preheat oven to 350 degrees. In a large mixing bowl, cream butter and sugar until lighter-colored and fluffy. Stir in dry ingredients and applesauce. Stir in raisins, dried cranberries and nuts. Pour into greased pan. Bake at 350 degrees for 60 minutes.

Date Nut Bread

*Moist date breads are a throwback to olden days. Always toast nuts before
you use them, especially the pecans you use in this recipe.
Toasting allows the nutty flavor to come through.*

1⅔ cups (10 ounces) pitted dates, chopped coarse
1 cup boiling water
1 teaspoon baking soda
2 cups all-purpose flour
¼ cup whole wheat flour
1 teaspoon baking powder
½ teaspoon salt
½ teaspoon nutmeg
Pinch ground cloves
1 cup vegetable oil
¾ cup dark brown sugar, packed
2 large eggs
⅔ cup buttermilk
2 teaspoons orange zest (zest of one orange)
1 cup walnuts or pecans, toasted, coarsely chopped

Preheat oven to 350 degrees. Stir dates, boiling water, and baking
soda together in a medium mixing bowl. Cover and set aside until
dates have softened, about 30 minutes. In a large bowl, whisk together
flours, baking powder, salt, and spices. In a medium bowl, whisk
brown sugar, buttermilk, oil, and eggs together until smooth, then stir
in date mixture until combined.

Gently fold buttermilk mixture into flour mixture with rubber spatula
until just combined. Do not over-mix. Fold in orange zest and nuts.
Fill greased and/or paper-lined loaf pans with batter and smooth tops.
Bake at 350 degrees on a rack positioned in the middle of the oven for
about 45-50 minutes, rotating pans halfway through baking, and until
golden brown and toothpick or skewer inserted in center comes out
with few crumbs attached. Cool in pan 20 minutes; turn out on wire
rack; cool an additional hour.

Zucchini Carrot Bread

Zucchini are the Mainland version of mangoes; when you have any, you have too many. That's how zucchini bread came into existence; the high water content in the cousin of the cucumber creates a moist bread.

1½ cup all-purpose flour
1 teaspoon salt
1 teaspoon baking powder
½ teaspoon baking soda
1 teaspoon cinnamon
½ teaspoon nutmeg
¼ teaspoon ginger
½ cup pecans or walnuts, chopped
¼ cup shredded coconut flakes
2 large eggs
1½ cups sugar
1 cup grated zucchini
1 cup grated carrots
½ cup vegetable oil
¼ cup water

Preheat oven to 350 degrees. Sift dry ingredients. Stir in nuts and coconut; set aside. Beat eggs and sugar until well mixed, but do not whip into a foam. Stir in the grated vegetable oil and water. Add egg mixture to the dry ingredients and mix just until combined. Divide into two loaf pans and bake at 350 degrees for 40-45 minutes, or when tested in the center, a toothpick comes out with few crumbs attached.

sweetendings

This collection of desserts is for times of indulgence. Many are more sophisticated and make lovely meal-enders, but remember to match the dessert to menu. If the dessert is very rich or heavy, the meal should be lighter; after a simple salad lunch, however, you're free to employ a more lavish hand.

The recipes here range from classics worthy of a professional pastry chef, to frozen desserts that require an ice cream maker; from candy (a bit tricky to make in our humid climate) to an old-fashioned oatmeal crumble even a child could toss together; from airy fruit-based desserts to Island favorite bread pudding.

Can't Let Go Cream Puffs

YIELD: 12 PUFFS

Don't be afraid of cream puffs: Pate choux dough is actually easy to make, just a matter of stirring vigorously. Or buy plain frozen cream puffs, defrost and use them, filling with ice cream, pudding or other good, soft things.

For the puff pastry (pate choux):
½ cup unsalted butter
1 cup water
⅛ teaspoon salt
1 teaspoon sugar
1 cup flour
4 eggs

For the filling:
3 ounces instant pudding (flavor of your choice)
1½ cup cold milk
8 ounces whipping cream

Make pate choux: Line a cookie sheet with cooking parchment. In a medium, heavy saucepan, bring butter, water, salt and sugar to a boil. Add flour all at once and whisk or stir to incorporate while cooking, until mixture becomes silky and forms a ball. Remove from heat and add eggs one at a time, stirring vigorously after each addition. Drop ¼ cup of batter onto parchment-lined cookie sheet. Bake at 375 degrees for 50 minutes until puffy and golden brown. Cool before filling.

Make the filling: Beat instant pudding and cold milk with mixer. Beat whipping cream until firm. Fold whipped cream into pudding mixture until well-blended. Fill cooled puffs with pastry bag and tip, or cut into puffs and fill bottom half; place top half on filling. Sprinkle with powdered sugar if desired.

Almond Walnut Butter Toffee

YIELD: ABOUT 28-32 PIECES

This sweet, rich, chewy, butter confection will appeal to children as well as adults and makes a great holiday gift. Be sure to use a candy thermometer (instant-read thermometers don't measure highly enough).

2¼ cups sugar
1¼ cups unsalted butter
½ cup water
1 teaspoon salt
1½ cups chopped blanched almonds (½ pound)
1 cup chopped walnuts (6 ounces)
6 ounces semi sweet chocolate (melted)

Combine sugar, butter, water and salt in a medium-size pot and bring to a boil over medium-high heat. Continue cooking, stirring constantly with wooden spoon, until mixture registers 325 degrees on candy thermometer. Stir in almonds and ½ cup of walnuts. Pour into generously greased pan, spreading evenly. Let cool, spread with melted chocolate and sprinkle with remaining walnuts.

Cut toffee into little cubes or break into small pieces.

Variation: *Use macadamia nuts, pecans.*

Wiggle & Jiggle
Coconut Gelatin

Granulated gelatin can be credited to Charles Knox, who invented it in 1894. Gelatin previously came in tricky sheets and, in any case, was tough to work with no reliable source of refrigeration. Cookbooks of the early 20th century were full of gelatin recipes as electric refrigerators proliferated.

5 cups water
7 ounces coconut cream powder
⅛ teaspoon salt
1½ cups sugar
6 packages gelatin
1 cup water

Bring 5 cups of water to a boil. Remove from heat; add salt and coconut cream powder. Stir until dissolved and smooth with a mixer. Add sugar. Dissolve gelatin in 1 cup water. Add to coconut mixture and mix thoroughly. When warm, pour in pan and chill. Before placing refrigerator stir again; otherwise, mixture will separate.

Sweet Pineapple Crumble

....

YIELD: 9 BY 9-INCH PAN

You can use old-fashioned oats for this crumble; they give a whole-bran, chewy crunch to the dessert. Rolled quick oats are okay, too, and they cook more rapidly. If you enjoy shopping at farmers markets, look for miniature, ultra-sweet sugar pines, or try Maui Gold, a variety also bred to be particularly low in acid.

7-9 cups pineapple, diced (1 medium pineapple)
2 cups oatmeal
1 cup brown sugar, firmly packed
¾ teaspoon cinnamon
¼ teaspoon baking soda
Pinch of ground cloves
¼ teaspoon salt
1½ sticks butter

Preheat oven to 350 degrees. In a large bowl, combine dry ingredients and toss together until thoroughly mixed and all the ingredients are incorporated. Add the melted butter and mix by hand until butter is incorporated and crumbly. Sprinkle an even layer of the crumble mixture on the bottom of the 9 by 9-inch pan and press lightly to form a crust. Add the spices to the diced pineapple, plus 2 cups of crumble mixture. Spread on the crumble layer in the pan. Finish with a layer of crumble mixture on top of the pineapples. Dot with butter. Place pan on a lined baking sheet pan to catch any spills. Bake at 350 degrees for 45 minutes or until fruit is bubbling and topping is brown. Any leftover crumble mixture can be frozen for later use.

Variation: *Use mango, peaches, Kula strawberries.*

Pineapple Surprise

This quick and simple dessert can be thrown together from ingredients you probably have on hand. Don't forget to keep the pineapple juice; the recipe needs it. If you've got pineapple chunks or slices, you can briefly pulse them in a food processor to stand in for crushed pineapple.

<u>For the crust:</u>
   ¾ cups unsalted butter
   1½ cups all-purpose flour
   ⅓ cups light brown sugar
   1 cup chopped macadamia nuts

<u>For the filling:</u>
   32 ounces sour cream
   12 ounces instant vanilla (four 3-ounce boxes)
   2 (20-ounce) cans crushed pineapple, in syrup
   Sweetened whipped cream for topping

Make the crust: Preheat oven to 350 degrees. Cream butter and sugar; add flour and nuts. Press in greased 9 by 13-inch pan. Bake at 350 degrees for 15 minutes, cool.

Make the filling: Blend pudding and sour cream. Add the crushed pineapple with the syrup. Spread mixture over cool crust and chill.

Top with sweetened whipped cream.

Variation: *Try walnuts, pecans.*

Kula Strawberry Ice Cream

YIELD: 10-12 SERVINGS

Sweet Kula strawberries are available year-round now (and we're getting berries from other islands, too). Do not make this with California imports; they won't lend the potent flavor and sweetness you want.

1 pound Kula strawberries,
   hulled and sliced thin, about
   3 cups
1¼ cups sugar
Pinch salt
1⅓ cups heavy cream
1¼ cups whole milk

6 large egg yolks, whisked in
   a bowl with ¼ cup of the
   sugar until smooth
3 tablespoons strawberry jam
1 teaspoon lemon juice
1 teaspoon vanilla extract

Combine strawberries and ½ cup sugar and salt in a bowl. Mash berries gently until slightly broken down. Let sit, stirring occasionally until juices have been extracted from the berries and sugar is dissolved, about 40-45 minutes. Combine cream, milk and ½ cup sugar in medium saucepan over medium-high heat, stirring occasionally until mixture reaches 175 degrees, about 5-10 minutes.

Remove from heat. Slowly whisk about half of the heated cream mixture into egg yolk mixture, ½ cup at a time. Return mixture to saucepan and cook over medium-low heat, stirring constantly until mixture thickens and registers 180 degrees, about 7-14 minutes.

Immediately strain custard through fine mesh strainer and let cool over bowl of ice water to room temperature, stirring occasionally.

While custard is cooling, transfer berries to a medium saucepan and simmer over medium-high heat, stirring occasionally until berries are softened and broken down, about 3 minutes. Add strawberry jam and dissolve.

Strain berries, reserving the juice. Transfer berries to a small bowl, stir in lemon juice and let cool to room temperature; cover and refrigerate until cold. Stir vanilla and reserved juice into custard; cover and refrigerate until custard reaches 40 degrees, at least 3 hours or up to 24 hours.

Pour custard into ice cream machine and churn until mixture resembles thick soft serve ice cream, about 25-30 minutes. Add berries; continue to churn until fully incorporated and berries are slightly broken down, about 1 minute. Transfer ice cream to air-tight container; press firmly to remove any air pockets and freeze until firm.

Tropical Fruit Medley with Honey Yogurt Sauce

YIELD: 6-8 SERVINGS

You can make this dessert with any mix of seasonal fruits and berries. Head to the farmers' market and try some of the newer tropical fruits. Use a good-quality natural yogurt or Greek yogurt.

<u>For the fruit (vary at will):</u>
   1 pineapple, peeled, cut into 1-inch cubes
   2 mangoes, peeled, cut into 1-inch cubes
   1 basket Kula strawberries, trimmed, cut in half
   1 basket blueberries
   1 basket raspberries
   3 kiwi, peeled and sliced
   1 can lychee, drained or equivalent fresh, peeled
   ½ bunch mint, thinly sliced

<u>For the sauce:</u>
   1 cup yogurt
   ¼ cup honey

Gently mix all fruits and mint leaves in a large bowl. Blend together honey and yogurt and drizzle over.

Ka'a'awa Bread Pudding

YIELD: 12 GENEROUS PIECES

This simple baked dessert is a member of the family of Island favorites: pudding made with egg custard and stale or dried bread, in this recipe; Portuguese pao doce (sweet bread).

1 (20-ounce) package Portuguese sweet bread, cubed
4½ cups milk
½ cup (1 stick) butter
1 cup sugar
½ can evaporated milk
2 teaspoons vanilla
4 eggs, slightly beaten
Cinnamon
Vanilla Cream Sauce (recipe on page 116)

Preheat oven to 350 degrees. Cube sweet bread and place in a 9 by 13-inch buttered pan. In a large pot, combine milk, butter, sugar, evaporated milk and vanilla. Bring to a slow boil. Remove and cool slightly. In a separate bowl, beat eggs slightly and slowly ladle the milk mixture into the eggs, stirring after each ladle-full so eggs do not scramble. Mix eggs and milk together and pour over cubed sweet bread. Sprinkle top generously with cinnamon. Bake at 350 degrees for 1 hour or more till set.

Variation: *Add ½ cup raisins.*

Vanilla Cream Sauce

1 quart whipping cream
½ cup golden brown sugar
1½ cups (3 sticks) butter
1 teaspoon vanilla extract

Melt butter and sugar in saucepan on medium heat for a few minutes, stirring constantly till slightly thickened. Add whipping cream and continue stirring till slightly thickened again. Remove from heat and add vanilla. Pour into squeeze bottle for serving (refrigerate leftover sauce, which is great for pancakes and waffles).

Hawaiian Vanilla
Ice Cream

You'll need some tools for making ice cream from scratch: an instant-read thermometer, an ice water bath made from a fine mesh strainer set over a medium bowl that is in turn set over a larger bowl of ice water and an ice cream machine. "Custard" is cook-talk for the cream-and-egg mixture that is the heart of ice cream.

1 Hawaiian vanilla bean
1½ cups whole milk
¾ cup sugar
⅛ teaspoon salt
6 large egg yolks, beaten in a bowl
2 cups heavy cream

Split vanilla bean lengthwise with a paring knife and remove seeds with the back of the blade. Place bean and seeds in a medium sauce pot and add the whole milk, sugar and salt. Bring to a simmer over medium low heat, stirring to dissolve sugar.

Slowly stir about 1 cup of the hot milk mixture into the beaten egg yolks. Then stir the egg mixture into the milk. Cook over low heat, stirring constantly with a heat proof spatula until custard reaches 175 degrees on the thermometer and coats the spatula blade. Do not boil! Strain immediately over an ice bath.

Refrigerate until cold or overnight. Stir in heavy cream and pour into ice cream maker and churn until mixture resembles thick soft serve ice cream, approximately 25-35 minutes.

Transfer ice cream to air tight container. Press firmly to remove any air pockets and freeze in ice cream maker until firm.

Chocolate Berry Shortcake

YIELD: 6 SHORTCAKES

*Nothing like old-fashioned strawberry shortcake, which tends to be overly
moist and sweet, this dessert combines a rich, chocolaty, cookie-like biscuit
with fresh fruit, which adds a nice acid balance, and whipped cream.
Use delectable Kula or other Island-grown strawberries
or other farmer's market fresh fruit as desired.*

For the biscuits:
1¼ cups pastry flour
6 ounces bittersweet chocolate, chopped
1 tablespoon baking powder
½ teaspoon salt
4 ounces butter, chilled, cubed
2 large eggs
¼ cup whole milk
½ cup sugar
¼ cup cocoa powder
Raw sugar for sprinkling

For the fruit:
4 cups berries, mashed or whole berries, sweetened or
    unsweetened
Chocolate Filling (recipe on page 120)
Easy Whipped Cream (recipe on page 121)
Vanilla Anglaise Sauce (recipe on page 123)

Preheat oven to 375 degrees. Line a baking tray with parchment paper.
Using a food processor combine flour, chocolate, baking powder and
salt. Add butter, process until mixture resembles a fine meal. In a
small bowl, whisk eggs and milk together. Add to the flour mixture,
pulse until combined. Scrape down bowl and beater. Do not over-mix.
Use an ice cream scoop to portion out biscuits, six 3-inch mounds,
on prepared baking sheet. Space evenly. Brush tops with milk and
sprinkle with raw sugar. Bake at 375 degrees for 15 minutes. Check for
doneness. Do not over-bake.

recipe continued on page 120

For the Chocolate Filling:
  ¼ stick (2 ounces) butter
  1 cup sugar
  ½ teaspoon salt
  1½ cups water
  3 tablespoons cocoa powder
  ½ cup water
  3 tablespoons cornstarch
  ¼ cup bitter or semi-sweet chocolate, chopped

In a sauce pot, bring butter, sugar, salt, cocoa powder and first water to a boil.

Combine second measure of water and cornstarch in a small bowl and make a slurry. Pour into boiling cocoa mixture whisking constantly until thickened. Bring to a boil and remove from heat when cornstarch is cooked out.

Add the chopped chocolate and stir until completely dissolved and incorporated into mixture. Cool. Cover with plastic wrap placing directly onto chocolate to prevent a skin from forming. Keep refrigerated till ready to assemble shortcakes. This mixture may be prepared the day before.

Easy Whipped Cream

2 cups heavy cream
2½ tablespoons powdered sugar
½ tablespoon vanilla extract

Combine all ingredients together and whip until stiff either by a hand mixer or in food processor. Use a piping bag fitted with a large tip if desired or simply spoon cream with an ice cream scoop or spoon.

....

To assemble shortcake: Split biscuits in half lengthwise. Place a scoop of chocolate filling, add berries on the bottom half of the biscuit. Dollop with whipped cream on the berries and add more berries on top of the cream. Place another small dollop of more whipped cream on the second layer of berries then secure the top on the dessert. Dust with powdered sugar if desired.

To plate: Place shortcake in center of plate and serve with Vanilla Anglaise Sauce if desired, or just use remaining fresh berries to garnish the plate.

Fresh Berries
with Vanilla Anglaise Sauce

Anglaise ("ahn-glaze"; French for "English") is nothing more than a loose custard, but remember that the simpler-sounding the recipe, the more difficult it's likely to be. To achieve the right rich smoothness, this sauce cannot be rushed and all the directions related to temperature must be followed to prevent the eggs from curdling or custard from thickening.

4 egg yolks
¼ cup sugar
1 cup half-and-half OR ½ cup whole milk and ½ cup cream
2 teaspoons vanilla extract
2 cups mashed or whole berries, sweetened or unsweetened

Set a fine mesh strainer over a medium bowl and set over a larger bowl of ice water to chill custard immediately once you've got the mixture made. Beat yolks together in a small mixing bowl and have ready for heated half-and-half mixture.

In a small sauce pot, bring half-and-half and sugar to a boil, then reduce to simmer. Carefully but quickly pour in about ½ cup of the hot mixture into the egg yolks, stirring constantly.

Pour the egg mixture into the simmering half-and-half, and stir with a heat-proof spatula. Use the thermometer and heat to 180 degrees. Mixture should coat the spatula. Do not boil.

Immediately pour mixture through strainer into bowl over ice water bath. Allow to cool; add vanilla and refrigerate until ready to use.

Serve over berries.

Kona Coffee Latte Gelee

Gelee (zhell-lay) is a cooked gelatin-like mixture that originated in France. Gelee-type desserts were very popular in the early years of the 20th century, when silky textured foods were considered to be the height of sophistication because they took the work of a skilled cadre of chefs. Make this one with a great Kona coffee, preferably 100 percent Kona.

2 packages plain gelatin
½ cup cold water
3 cups fresh-brewed, strong Kona Coffee,
   espresso or French Roast
½ cup half-and-half or heavy cream
¼ cup sugar or more to taste
Sweetened whipped cream for topping
Grated chocolate bar or cinnamon for garnish

In a large bowl, sprinkle gelatin over water and stir to moisten. Let it sit for 5 minutes to bloom. Combine sugar and hot coffee together and dissolve. Add half-and-half or heavy cream and stir to combine. Pour into 6 coffee cups and refrigerate until set, at least 2 hours.

Top with sweetened whipped cream. Sprinkle grated chocolate or cinnamon or cream for garnish. Serve with cookies, if desired.

Glossary

Almond paste – A pastry filling made with ground almonds or almond meal and sugar, then bound together with cooking oil, eggs, and heavy cream or corn syrup. Similar to marzipan, but with less sugar. Can be found in the baking section of a grocery store, but can also be easily homemade.

Anglaise – A loose custard.

Coconut cream powder – The powdered form of coconut cream.

Coconut milk – The juice from the meat of a coconut.

Craisins – Sugared, dried cranberries.

Fine baking sugar – Also called "super fine," it is regular (granulated) sugar that has been ground finely and produces a smoother texture in the finished product. Can be substituted for regular sugar. Not the same as powdered (confectioners' sugar).

Frangipane – A tart lined with almond paste.

Gelee – A cooked gelatin-like mixture that originated in France.

Haupia – A traditional Hawaiian coconut milk-based dessert often found at lū'aus.

Jalapeño – A medium-sized green chili pepper.

Kabocha pumpkin – A Japanese variety of winter squash.

Kalamansi – Philippines lime, a very tart citrus fruit, small and green to bright orange in color.

Katakuriko – Potato starch used to thicken soups or dust ingredients for deep-frying.

Kinako – Soybean flour.

Kirschwasser – A tart cherry liqueur made in the Schwarzwalder ("black forest"), southern Germany.

Ladyfingers – Light and sweet, finger-shaped sponge cake.

Li hing mui – Salty, dried plum. "Li hing" means "traveling" and "mui" means "plum."

Li hing powder – The powder is made by grinding up the skin of the plum that has been pickled in aspartame, food coloring, salt, and sugar. Can also be found at local-style "crack seed" snack shops.

Li hing prunes – Stewed prunes preserved with a li hing powder; can be homemade or found in local-style "crack seed" snack shops.

Macadamia nuts – A rich, flavorful nut, originally from Australia.

Miso – A Japanese seasoning made with fermented rice, barley and/or soybeans.

Mochi – Glutinous Japanese rice cakes.

Mochiko – Japanese name for glutinous rice flour.

Piña colada – A cocktail made with rum, cream of coconut, and pineapple juice.

Semolina flour – Coarse, purified wheat middlings.

Splenda – Artificial sugar.

Tiramisu – A dessert generally made with coffee-soaked ladyfinger.

Recipe Index

A

A is for Apple Pie, 81
Almond Walnut Butter Toffee, 104
Apple Frangipane Tart, 87
Applesauce Bread, 97

B

Baked Mochi with Miso, 40
Basler Brunsli, A Chocolate Nut
    Cookie, 33
Black Forest Cake Cupcake, 77
Brownie Points, 44
Butter Frosting, 74
Butter Shortbread Cookies, 18

C

Can't Let Go Cream Puffs, 103
Chilly Pear Dessert, 48
Chocolate Berry Shortcake, 118
Chocolate Chip Cookies, 24
Chocolate Covered Sugar Cookie, 34
Cinnamon Apple Cake, 54
Cinna-Yum Cinnamon Rolls, 6
Coconut Lovers Shortbread, 16
Cranberry Pecan Muffins, 8
Crunchy Banana Muffins, 3
Crunchy Oatmeal Cookies, 28
Custard Pie, 82

D

Date Nut Bread, 98

E

Easy Beer Bread, 96
Easy Chi Chi Mochi, 41
Easy Chocolate Coffee Mug Cake, 56
Easy Whipped Cream, 121

F

Fluffy Kirschwasser Frosting, 78
Forbidden Fudge Muffins, 10
Fresh Berries with Vanilla Anglaise
    Sauce, 123
Fruit Squares, 39
Fudge Cookies, 27

G

German Chocolate Cake, 59
Got Coffee Cake?, 65
Guava Frangipane Tartlets, 85
Guava Marbled Cheesecake, 63

H

Happy Almond Cookies, 22
Haupia Chocolate Cream Pie, 90
Hawaiian Vanilla Ice Cream, 117
Hot Date with Chocolate, 45
Hot Potato Rolls, 94

I

It's a Fruit Cake Bar, 47
It's All About Sweet Sugar Biscuits, 14
Italian Tozzetti Cookies

J

Johnny Apple Scones, 4
Jungle Monkey Bread, 93

K

Ka'a'awa Bread Pudding, 115
Kalamansi "7 Minute" Meringue Icing, 70
Kalamansi Cupcake, 69
Kona Coffee Latte Gelee, 124
Kula Strawberry Ice Cream, 110

M

Mango Cake, 75
Mango Upside Down Cake, 62
Mochiko Shortbread, 19

O

Open Sesame Seed Shortbread, 21

P

Papaya Pineapple Fruit Butter, 95
Peanut Butter Cookies, 29
Peter, Peter, Pumpkin Cake, 71
Piña Colada Pound Cake, 57
Pineapple Butter Sponge Bars, 49
Pineapple Surprise, 109
Pucker Up, Prune Apple Cake, 60

Pumpkin Chiffon, 88
Pumpkin Haupia Squares, 52

R

Red Velvet Cupcakes, 72
Russian Tea Cookies, 36

S

Simple Pie Crust, 80
Simply a Biscuit, 13
Some Like it HOT! Popovers, 11
Sweet Cornmeal Muffins, 5
Sweet Pineapple Crumble, 107

T

Temptin' Rugelach, 50
Tiramisu, 66
Tropical Fruit Medley with Honey Yogurt Sauce, 112

V

Vanilla Cream Sauce, 116

W

White Chocolate Chip Macadamia Nut Cookies, 25
Wiggle & Jiggle Coconut Gelatin, 106
Wild Blondies, 42

Z

Zucchini Carrot Bread, 100

Index

A

almonds, 27, 33, 36, 87, 104
 extract, 22, 87
 paste, 50, 85-86
apple, 3-4, 24, 39, 54, 60, 81
 jelly, 87
applesauce, 97
apricots, 34

B

banana, 3
beer, 96
berries, 110-112, 118, 121, 123
biscuits, 13-14, 93, 118, 121
Bisquick, 5
blueberries, 4, 42, 112
buttermilk, 59, 93, 98

C

candied fruit, 47
carrots, 100
cherries, 47
 Maraschino, 77
 pie filling, 77
chocolate, 33, 45, 51, 56, 59, 66, 77, 90,
 104, 118, 120-121, 124
 baking, 10, 24, 59, 118
 bittersweet, 118
 candy bar, 77, 124
 chips, 24-25, 27-28, 45, 56
 dark, 34, 44
 semi-sweet chips, 24, 27, 56
 pudding mix, 90
 unsweetened, 44
 white chips, 25, 27

cinnamon,
 3-4, 6-7, 30,
 33, 39, 48,
 50-52, 54,
 60, 65, 71,
 75, 81, 88,
 93, 97, 100, 107,
 115, 124
cloves, 98, 107
cocoa powder, 33, 56,
 72, 77, 118, 120
coconut, 16, 28
 cream powder, 106
 flakes, 59
 milk, 40-41, 52, 57, 90
 shredded, 16, 28, 57, 75, 100
coffee, Kona, 66, 124
corn syrup, 33, 70, 78
cornflakes, 75
cornstarch, 52, 63, 90, 120
craisins, 7, 28, 42
cranberries, 7-8, 28, 42, 48, 97
cream
 cream, 48, 50, 63
 heavy, 4, 110, 117, 121, 124
 of tartar, 70, 78
 whipped, 66, 88, 90, 103, 109, 118,
  121, 124
 whipping, 66, 103, 116

D

dates, 28, 45, 98
Disaronno Amaretto Liqueur, 30

F

flour
- cake, 6, 13, 49, 57, 59, 69, 72, 85-86
- mochi, 40
- pastry, 118
- semolina, 62
- wheat, 19, 96, 98
fruit filling, 39

G

gelatin, 88, 106, 124
ginger, 100
graham cracker pie crust, 63
guava
- jam, 85
- juice, 63

H

Hawaiian vanilla bean, 117
hazelnuts, 30, 33
heavy cream, 4, 110, 117, 121, 124
honey, 112

K

kalamansi zest, 69-70
katakuriko, 40-41
kinako, 40
Kirschwasser, 77-78
kiwi, 112

L

ladyfingers, 66
lemon, 39, 47
- extract, 57
- juice, 57, 110-111
- zest, 8, 33
li hing prunes, 60
lychee, 112

M

macadamia nuts, 8, 10, 18-19, 24-25, 27, 42, 44-45, 48, 51, 65, 97, 104, 109
mango, 62, 75, 95, 107
mascarpone cheese, 66
mashed potatoes, 94

milk, 5-8, 13-14, 40-41, 54, 56-57, 62, 72, 74, 77, 81-82, 88, 94, 103
  condensed, 27, 63
  evaporated, 52, 59, 115
  low fat, 90
  sweetened condensed, 27, 63
  whole, 11, 110, 117-118, 123
mint, 56, 112
miso, 40
mochiko, 19, 41

N

nutmeg, 14, 52, 60, 81-82, 88, 97-98, 100

O

oats, 28, 96, 107
orange, 47, 56, 69, 98
  rind, 56
  zest, 98

P

peanut butter, 29
pears, 4, 48
pecans, 8, 10, 24, 27, 33, 36, 42, 44-45, 59-60, 98, 100, 104, 109
pie shell, 88, 90
pineapple, 49, 57, 86, 94-95, 107, 109, 112
Portuguese sweet bread, 115
pudding, 90, 103, 109, 115
pumpkin, 52, 71, 81, 88, 97
  purée, 52

R

raisins, 6-7, 28, 50-51, 75, 97, 115
raspberries, 112
  jam, 50

S

sesame seeds, 21
shortening, 8, 13, 22, 80, 94
sour cream, 57, 65, 69, 72, 109
strawberries, 4, 118
  Kula, 107, 110, 112
  jam, 95, 110-111
sweetened condensed milk, 27, 63

V

vanilla, 3, 6, 10, 14, 19, 24-25, 27, 34, 36, 42, 44, 48, 50, 52, 54, 56-57, 59, 62-63, 65, 69, 72, 74-75, 77, 82, 90, 97, 109-111, 115-116, 118, 121, 123
  Hawaiian vanilla bean, 117

W

walnuts, 3, 8, 10, 24, 27, 33, 36, 42, 44-45, 47, 50, 60, 65, 75, 98, 100, 104, 109
whipped cream, 66, 88, 90, 103, 109, 118, 121, 124
whipping cream, 66, 103, 116

Y

yeast, 6-7, 94
yogurt, 112

Z

zucchini, 97, 100